Recuerdos de mi Barrio

by

Ramón Francisco Villarreal

authorHOUSE®

AuthorHouse™
1663 Liberty Drive, Suite 200
Bloomington, IN 47403
www.authorhouse.com
Phone: 1-800-839-8640

First published by AuthorHouse 1/4/2008

ISBN: 978-1-4343-5827-1 (sc)

Library of Congress Control Number: 2007910170

Printed in the United States of America
Bloomington, Indiana

This book is printed on acid-free paper.

DEDICATION

This book is dedicated to family members who will now have a memory of relatives and events that they might not otherwise have known. Additionally, it is dedicated to immediate family without whom I would not likely have undertaken this project. Finally it is in appreciation to those who gave me guidance in clarifying parts of this manuscript and whose editorial contributions helped me clarify my own thoughts and memories.

Acknowledgements

There are several people I want to acknowledge for their support and contributions. The task of compiling all of this information, as it turned out, was bigger than I originally anticipated. Somehow, the idea became a project that required research beyond my memories.

After discussions with immediate family and other relatives, I sat down and wrote and wrote as far as my memory took me.

It was at this stage—the completion of my initial writings—that I turned over the project to Leo Cárdenas, a friend of more than three decades, a fellow civil rights warrior and more importantly, published author and former newspaper and magazine editor. It was Leo, who not only dotted the *i's* and crossed the *t's*, but arranged all of my recollections and childhood stories into topics—the family, World War II, the influence of the railroad, our neighbors, the food we ate and how we cooked it and the feasts and holidays we celebrated. We felt that historians, people who lived during this decade and the curious reader would find it more interesting this way.

Working with Leo also gave us an unexpected but rewarding surprise. We found that we are separated in age by only four months, and as a result, had more commonalties that we had realized.

We found, for example, that even though he was raised in Del Rio, Texas, some 900 miles and two states from my hometown of Pratt, Kansas, we were affected by similar cultures involving food, customs, traditions and language of the 1940s. We didn't meet until we both worked for the U.S. Community Relations Service (CRS) in 1971. We were both 36 years old then.

And the most common denominator, we found, was our ancestors. In both cases, our families came from Mexico in the 1910-20s, both fleeing the Mexican Revolution, and bringing with them customs, traditions, culture, language and hope for a better future.

TABLE OF CONTENTS

Acknowledgements	**vii**
Prologue	**xiii**
Part One: The Family	**1**
Faces and Names	3
Kansas, my Kansas	4
In the Middle of Nowhere	5
Saddest day, saddest trip	7
Huge as in Big Man	8
Geographic Details	11
The Villarreal Compound	14
Two garages like bookends	16
Of tools and sheds	17
And even a caboose	18
Pets and Varmints	19
El molino de viento	20
The mighty Honey Locust	24
Cement Blocks	26
Beginning of formal education	28
A shoeshine stand	30
So we tried construction	30
The Wedding	31
What, no television?	33
A real bull story	38
A call from nature	39
Face the música	40
Adivinanzas	41

Television Finally Came to the Barrio   42

Días de Caza   43

Waterfowl in Kansas   44

A big black dog   46

Dog Number 2   47

Don Leobardo   48

My cousins   49

Extended family and other cultural relationships   50

Part Two: The Railroad and World War II   **53**

The Railroad Influence   55

A Dangerous Job   59

The cantaloupe accident   61

World War II   62

College was out of the question   65

Part Three: Unforgettable Neighbors   **67**

Our favorite neighbors   69

Nicknames and Sobrenombres   70

El Gallito   71

Clarita: la no muy bonita   72

Our own "Fats"   73

And then there was Vic   74

One more brother   76

The Flea could play   77

Raccoon Captor   80

El Mocho   81

From A to Z: Still Weird   81

White family in the barrio   84

A rock by any name   86

Thirty bales of hay 87

Swimming in a sandpit 88

Visitas: Roll your own cigarettes 90

Doña Mariquita 91

Don Pedro and Doña Mercedes 92

Don Teófilo 94

Some White folks 96

Los Pérsicos 97

John Deere tractor 100

A large migrant family 100

Bennie gets nailed 104

Don José and Doña Rosa 106

Tinkers and tailors 108

The circus is in town 109

The Medicine Show 111

Riding in a parade float 113

Boy Scouts at work 114

El Caballo Blanco 115

The day the cows came home alone 116

House moving and other events 117

The flood in the potato patch 119

Paving the way 120

Tragedy in the barrio 122

An un-neighborly family 123

Cruising down Main Street 126

How not to be in the local newspaper 127

Part Four: Feast Days and Food   **131**

Feast Days 133

Christmas and Tamales   133

New Year's Eve   137

Chile not chili   139

La cuaresma   141

The Mobile Market   143

The Watermelon Man   143

Outside help   145

Part Five: The End of an Era   **147**

Unwelcome return   149

The last family in the barrio   150

Changes in the barrio   152

End of an era   154

Epilogue   **157**

Former Residents Long Gone   **159**

Endnotes   **161**

About the Author   **165**

PROLOGUE

If a tree falls in the forest and nobody hears it, does it make a sound?

Many have pondered this question for many years.

I've struggled with a more compelling controversy:

If a neighborhood virtually disappears from the vast plains of rural Kansas, does anybody care?

In today's highly technological world of computer and the Internet, this dilemma has been stated in another way:

If a tree falls in a forest and *Google* doesn't index it, is it actually published?

I've decided that I am not going to wait for *Google* for an answer.

My research and my memories of the *barrio*[1]—the neighborhood--where I grew up can no longer be ignored. The barrio has literally been erased from this face of the earth, but the pictures of that neighborhood of about one hundred people are still very vivid.

So I have decided to tell you about it.

Life in a *barrio* in the 1940s and early 1950s in Pratt, Kansas was quite different from mainstream mid-America. Along with other Kansans, we experienced hot summers and heavy snow and freezing cold during most winters. Our houses were not insulated for the first 12 years of my life and when we finally did insulate, it was only rock wool in the attic. The walls of the houses were boards with small gaps between them. When we modernized the house, we added a siding with some insulation but not enough to keep out the bitter cold of Kansas's severe winters.

We tolerated the summer heat as there was no air conditioning available until the mid-1950s, and even then, it would have required central heating and expensive retrofitting. In the early years, summer cooling consisted of cross ventilation meaning a window open on opposite sides of the house and dwindling expectations of getting a breeze.

With the many thunderstorms that we had on late afternoons, it also meant closing the windows once the strong wind gusts arrived driving the cold rain and blowing the dust that preceded the rain.

In later years, window units, evaporative coolers, that used water and a squirrel cage fan, cooled the house but not to a really comfortable level. Moreover, these coolers made the furniture and the whole house feel clammy and probably helped mold to grow unseen throughout the house.

Barrios were a common sight in the early years of the last century but there are still several *barrios* in many cities and larger towns along the Mexican border. *Barrios* varied much like other neighborhoods in cities but while these had names such as *El Santo Niño* and names of saints or the *Virgin María*, ours had no name.

It was just "*el barrio.*"

Living in the *barrio* meant just one sure thing—poverty. There were no *barrios* anywhere that I can remember that would have been considered middle class much less rich. In smaller towns with a Hispanic population there was usually only one barrio. Wealthier Hispanics were sprinkled among the rest of the population in most cities, as they become financially able to move into middle class neighborhoods.

In today's more modern world, Hispanics, especially Mexicans, are scattered throughout upscale neighborhoods if they can afford it.

Redlining, a real estate practice that caused Hispanics to not secure home loans in neighborhoods that did not allow them, still exists but Hispanics who can afford to move out of the *barrio* can do so more easily now than in the past.

Poorer Hispanics, largely migrants and persons engaged in seasonal or other low pay work, are concentrated in farm areas. Many work in agriculture or related activities and live in less than desirable housing in many places worse than the poorer barrios.

In cities today there are *informal barrios*, that is, neighborhoods that are being inherited from old residents that sell the old house and move to a *whiter* neighborhood or in some cases, move to live out their retirement years with relatives elsewhere.

In our *barrio* there were many families that lived and died long before I was born. I am writing about those that I can still remember and one or two features that are ingrained in my memory. Even today, I still fight not to remember some *barrio* dwellers. In my senior years, I have tried to erase negative memories, but then I would not be giving you a true and more balanced picture if I left out the negative parts of the *barrio*.

My parents left me with one everlasting value. That is to treat everyone with respect. So throughout this book, I have referred to family and neighbors with the endearing terms of *Don* and *Doña*. These are terms of respect.

The terms *Don* is used with the first name of a gentleman, and *Doña* with the first name of a lady. I will also use *el* for the masculine and *la* for the feminine when addressing individuals by their nicknames. So you will get to meet individuals with nicknames or *apodos such as el Mocho, el Sapo, la Bruja, el Gordo, el Güero, el Gallito* (a female with a masculine nickname), *el Chale* and *el Jorobado*. There are persons whose real name I did not know at one time but now simply remember them by the nicknames we used.

Barrio conditions in my youth were not primitive although we had no indoor plumbing until around 1954. Outhouses were predominantly "two-holers," a term that is not well known today except perhaps, for campers or those who grew up in similar surroundings. Houses were dependent on coal or wood fired-heaters known as potbellied stoves.

Since well-to-do families did not live in the *barrio* there was no political pressure on city government to pave our streets or to provide city services. Finally in the mid -1950s, after I had graduated from high school, the *barrio* was connected to city utilities such as natural gas, water and sewer.

Life was different in other parts of the town. White families who lived *uptown,* that is closer to the center of town, enjoyed paved streets, which were swept weekly. These homes had all the utilities. Houses on Main Street were more opulent and usually belonged to bankers and other business owners. These also sported well maintained landscaping.

Periodically, usually prior to city elections, city crews graded the barrio's dirt streets to garner the votes for the mayor or other incumbents running for re-election. In contrast, the south end of the town--the neighborhood where black folks lived-- had city amenities from the earliest times that I can recall, long before WWII. This section was actually part of the city whereas the barrio was considered as a separate entity, much like an unwanted suburb. Even the name "Walker's Addition" denoted separation.

The "colored"(the term that was used then) section of town, the south end close to the Santa Fe railroad tracks, had a swimming pool, a park with playground equipment and several businesses including restaurants, barbecue "joints," car repair garages and other establishments. Fortunately they did not have enough students for a separate segregated school or they would likely have been thus categorized.

The Santa Fe railroad had only a minor line to town on which they served the few industries in that area, primarily one wheat elevator and a few merchants receiving freight from the larger cities on the Santa Fe system. The elevator stored wheat from the south of the city but did not generate much business as most of the wheat fields were north of town where the large elevators were located and the Rock Island Railroad serviced them.

The main line of the Rock Island Railroad was at the north end of the city, where we lived. It was the Rock Island Railroad that determined the livelihood of those who lived in the *barrio*. The rail line connected the Midwest with the West Coast and had a lot of freight traffic. The large grain elevators there had two tracks where trains could load wheat, the principal farm crop of this area, for shipment to the east and west coasts and, perhaps, other countries from the connection with barges and ships.

This railroad action attracted transients, who came through periodically but worked for their food. Whenever a hobo showed up in the *barrio*, he was fed and given a "to go" bag of food for the rest of his trip by rail.

Most of these traveling men said they were going to California to seek their fortune. Unfortunately, this was in the 1940s, not the 1840s, so they may never have struck gold.

All of these travelers were non-Hispanic. Mexican *Braceros* did come through but usually on the way to work in western Kansas engaging in migratory and seasonal farm work. A few did stay a little while in the *barrio* working for food and shelter. They remained a week or two then moved on. We knew nothing about "green cards" at this time and assumed that they were legal immigrants. In any event, it was not a major issue in this era.

During this period no one would have cared about their status since they were willing to work at hard jobs like chopping wood for the cook stove and for heating the house during the winter. The *barrio* was safe haven for hobos who could come down from the railroad yards and enjoy a meal with a resident and put in a few minutes of work at chores that the young folks would otherwise have to do. Following the feast at one of the homes in the *barrio*, the hobo would return to the yard and hop a freight train going west.

Their life was not glamorous as depicted in movies but was fairly dangerous. "Riding the rods" was a dangerous way to travel. It did not require a ticket and was very low fare but subject to a beating by the "railroad bull," a policeman hired by the railroad to protect railroad property. This protection included getting the free riders off trains if he happened to catch them.

Many of these hobos talked about particularly vicious railroad bulls in certain railroad yards like Argentine or Armourdale, both in the Kansas City, Kansas area. Hobos have disappeared from society. In the days when they came through the *barrios* of Kansas, they moved on and some may have eventually found jobs and settled down.

Years ago, I heard, there was am annual hobo festival somewhere in Iowa. I assume that the festival helped the hobos get rid of their wandering stigma.

For the first five years of my life I lived in a Spanish-speaking environment. Spanish was the language of the *barrio* and even though my parents and uncles all spoke English at work or in town, they did not do so at home. The older generation did not speak English anywhere although they probably understood more than we thought at the time.

Most of the families in the *barrio* lived in small crowded houses with usually three and, sometimes, four generations living under one roof. The definition of *extended family* was well defined in the *barrio*. Residents were primarily second-generation descendents of immigrants from Mexico. There were also a few older and retired immigrants.

Every one in my extended family ate in the kitchen in the main house, which sported the customary wood burning stove, but was stoked mainly with coal. It heated water for cooking purposes. A wash boiler, a large racetrack shaped copper vessel, served to heat water for other purposes, such as washing dishes and clothes, and bathing. All of our household water came from a deep well that utilized a windmill to draw the cool, clear, refreshing water from the depths of the earth.

Members of the household had daily chores and for the men, who all worked for the railroad, this meant a very long workday.

My brother, my sister and I all had chores starting at a young age. The chores were not heavy at first or very complicated but did increase in scope and complexity, as we got older. Typical chores involved feeding the chickens or the pig, hauling in coal for the stoves, chopping wood and other yard and household chores. Shoveling snow was mostly a seasonal chore.

The farmyards in our rural area included a barn, a machine shed and other buildings such as a shed for calves and a hog pen. *Barrio* yards were similar in some ways and included, at a minimum, a well with a pumping mechanism from a windmill, an electric motor or good old hand power.

Some houses had garages built on the property but away from the house. There were not many cars in the *barrio* so these garages served mainly as shelters for dogs and storage for firewood. Only one garage in the barrio had a cement floor, all others were dirt floors and quite dusty.

Unlike today's homes with small yards, virtually all houses in the *barrio* had large yards with gardens, and several outbuildings.

Finally, a word on some of the hard decisions I had to make to complete this goal. By design, I have narrowed the history of these stories to the decade of 1940-50. I turned six in 1941, and it was then that I literally opened my eyes to my small but very interesting world. It so happened that two major events, World War II and the eventual demise of railroad operations in my hometown, occurred in this decade. Both events had a lasting and dramatic impact on all those people that I grew up with, including my immediate family.

And, indeed World War II not only changed my tiny slice of this country but affected all of us in many ways.

This, then, is what was happening in rural Kansas in the 1940s to several Hispanic families whose ancestors had fled Mexico to escape a revolution and loss of virtually all their material possessions. They subsequently found themselves contributing immensely to the future of a new adopted country.

PART ONE

THE FAMILY

Todo lo que hacíamos
era para la familia.
*--**Mi Madre***

Everything we did
was for the family.
*--**My Mom***

FACES AND NAMES

Anchondo. Argomedo. Blea.

The names are ingrained in memory.

Caraveo. Cervantes. Chacón. Crollet.

Not in alphabetical order. Of course not.

Durán. Encinias. Flores. García. Gonzales.

Each name had a face. Actually, many faces. These are the last names of the people I grew up with.

Maldonado. Martínez. Mena, Montaño. Navarro. Palacios.

Some of the faces have wrinkles. Most of the faces are smooth as the shell of an egg I have just picked up by putting my hand under the hen and whispering "shoo" and thinking it's okay with the hen. These are the ever-young faces of the kids in the *barrio*.

Rojas. Ramírez. Saenz. Valverde.

Actually, and to be honest, I don't really remember the faces by their last names.

It's nicknames, and in some cases, their first names, that come to my computer mind screen.

I didn't need a computer mind screen to see the faces then. Every thing just happened the way it was supposed to be. One day there was a new baby in the neighborhood, and the new baby's arrival somehow seemed to coincide with the funeral my folks attended the previous week.

Villarreal.

Villarreal. Villarreal. Villarreal.

No need to guess. That's my apellido, surname. My family's surname. It still shouts at me whenever I think of it in terms of a last name, a family. In reality, many families, some tied quite closely without knots, others bumping into each other as if in a bowl of molasses. Still others like tumbleweeds waiting for the wind to carry it to a new location.

Truth be known, *Villarreal* brings a very warm feeling that starts somewhere in my head and travels gingerly throughout my body and down to the bottom of my feet. Then—always, yes, always-- I wrapped the name, all ten letters, in my chest, put my arms around it and hold it tightly.

Villarreal.

That's the story I want to tell. But in order to tell you about all the other families, for after all, whether I want to admit it or not, they all had something to do in the molding of the individual that I have become.

I also need to tell you that this is the *barrio* as I remembered it. Whenever I get together with my brother and sister, we, naturally go back to our childhood and relive things that happened to us. We **don't** always remember these events in the same way nor did we see the people in the *barrio* the same way.

KANSAS, MY KANSAS

Whenever I tell people I meet for the first time that I was born in Kansas, they don't seem to accept this fact very well. Although they don't tell me to my face—at least, not right away—their faces want to blare out:

"I didn't know there were that many Hispanics[2] (or Latinos or Mexicans) in Kansas."

And they are right. Today only about 7 percent of Kansas population is Hispanic or Latino out of the 2.6 plus million citizens. And that in itself is remarkable and due mainly, I believe, because of the latest wave of immigrants and the jobs, both in farms and in urban areas, that not only Kansas offers but the whole United States.

That's how we, the Villarreals, came to Kansas, to work.

But it was neither the farms nor any construction boom that brought us.

It was the railroad. It was the Rock Island railway line. And to a lesser degree, the Santa Fe Railroad Company that most folks are familiar with.

My recollection of Kansas, my Kansas, starts around 1941. Since I was born in the seventh month of year when all the talk around our house was just how cold the weather had been and how hot it was now, I was actually looking forward to going to school later that year. That's because all the kids talked about then was what happened in Sacred Heart Catholic School and how mean the nuns were. Not true, "If you behaved."

I can still see all the faces that made up my *barrio*-- About 100, from dark brown to light tan, to real *güeros*[3] with light colored hair. But mostly the faces were somewhat brown, dark tan in the summers, and light again in the winters. All except the two Negro (that's what we called them then) families and the two white families.

Since we outnumbered them around 100 to 4, I thought that the world pretty much was us. We spoke Spanish all the time. We understood each other well. We went to town on most Saturdays and to church all Sundays, no matter what the weather, and if there was something else beyond that and other people "out there" we didn't know much about that. And that was all right. Then.

IN THE MIDDLE OF NOWHERE

The best way to direct you to my *barrio,* the home of some fond adventures and some tragedies, is to the intersection of U.S. Highway 54, which runs east and west, and U.S. Highway 281, which runs north and south. And that's pretty much in the center of Kansas, just a lot, quite a lot, toward the south end of the state.

That's the home of Pratt, Kansas. Just not exactly our hometown. But close.

We came from what folks call the outskirts of the town, the other side of the tracks, the poor part of town.

This pretty much confirms what I've been trying to convey to you. That I came from and grew up in the *barrio.*

Today, the population of Pratt is about 6,570. In 1940 it was 10,000+, including all 100 or so of us *barrio folks.*

Five miles north of Pratt is Iuka. Sawyer is eleven miles to the south; Medicine Lodge is the town just beyond Sawyer. And if you are still heading south after that, well, you're going to Oklahoma and we just never talked about going to Oklahoma although we did pass through on the way to Mexico or Texas to visit relatives.

The big city of Wichita is less than 100 miles to the east of Pratt. I just never went there when I was small but I heard my father and mother and my uncles and aunts talk about their trips. I did finally go there while in grade school when we played in the annual Diocesan basketball tournament at the Cathedral gym. Another larger city of note was Hutchinson, a place I did not visit until my teenage years. It was well known for the salt mines under the city.

We grew our own vegetables. We hunted for meat. In the summers when the growing season was at its highest, we waited for Don Alfredo to come around with his truck and trailer with watermelons and cantaloupes.

We were pretty much a little, very little, world of our own. We depended on our own family first and then to the other families around us.

But pretty much we just worked. All of us. It didn't matter how old you were or whether you were a boy, a girl, a teen, married or single. You worked. You had to work, to do your part, to keep the *barrio* going and vibrant.

The center of our universe was the Rock Island Railroad with the roundhouse near our homes much like a lighthouse looking over the landscape, about a quarter mile from our house on the north end of town. Every adult man and some teens, who were big and strong and lied about their age worked for the railroad on the section gang or at the roundhouse.

There were about ten or twelve families depending on the census or informal grouping. We all lived in two, three and four room frame houses. If a household had less than ten people living in it, well, that was a rarity. A rarity that didn't last long before a boarder or two moved in.

We shared veggies with each other, for we always seemed to have enough. And, we always took care of our hobos, who were constantly traveling through our area. We made sure they got a good meal to keep them from starving. We then allowed them to chop wood or do some other manual work. They usually got a packed lunch before they hopped on the next train out.

No one ever went hungry in our *barrio.*

SADDEST DAY, SADDEST TRIP

On a typical January day in Kansas, just days after the world had greeted the new millennium, I returned to the *barrio* after having been gone for some years. Snow still covered the barren earth and the grasslands, temperatures were in the mid-20s but with the frigid wind blowing, it felt much colder and sadder than I ever remembered.

Perhaps, the cold that penetrated my overcoat came not so much from the low temperature and the wind but from the occasion.

We had returned to Pratt, to the *barrio,* and to the community cemetery to bury my mother, our matriarch.

Doña Maria Nieves Maldonado de Villarreal had come home for the last time to our *barrio*—and to join her husband, Don Ramón Faustino Villarreal Quiñones, my father and our family's patriarch. She was only a few days short of 88 years of age, born 12/28/1912, died 12/21/2000.

My father had been waiting for her for a long time. He was just 55 years old when he died in 1963, a victim of lung cancer, born 2/15/1908, died 8/9/63.

While there had never been any mystery as where my parents—or me and really, all of us—would wind up, the cemetery or in a flower-decorated ceramic vase, the end of the priest's prayers, the placing of the roses on the casket, and our silent tears brought closure to the role of the Villarreal family in the Kansas plains in many ways.

All I had to do was look around me. The headstones with names like Chacón, Chabolla, Cobos, Maldonado and Navarro appeared to stare back at me. Not the headstones, but the faces and the memories of the owners of those faces that I had known so well. Some brought inner smiles, even a soft laugh. Others jerked at my gut, for there were many times I didn't agree with my playmates on events that now bore more on vandalism than jokes.

After the service I drove my family to the *barrio*. I wanted all of us to see one more time where I had grown up.

We were greeted by a desolate piece of land. Weeds had broken through the snow in search of sun and oxygen in some places. For a long time I glanced to the east, a very familiar direction hoping to get a glimpse of the roundhouse of the Rock Island railroad. It was not to be. It, too, was gone, having been torn down years before.

Where were the houses? Where were children?

What happened to *el Mocho, el Sapo?* And *la bruja?* They were nowhere to be found. Surely, with all the magical powers we attributed to *la bruja* in those days, surely, she would be there.

Gone without a trace. All gone.

All gone, all right. Except taxes.

Today there are no buildings in the old family compound. It is merely a vacant area that consists of two lots on which we pay property taxes to the city and county. Even the stately tall trees are gone. The lots do not reflect anything of what used to be there while we were growing up.

It was there and then that I made a promise to myself. A promise that I would not allow the memory of those days to be erased forever. If my family and my neighbors still lived in center of my brain, then I could bring back the times that mother time had wiped away from that part of the Kansas plains.

This is the fulfillment of my promise.

HUGE AS IN BIG MAN

On a pleasant November day when the sun warmed our bodies just enough to be comfortable, our family gathered in what we considered our living room to enjoy the most enjoyable part of our day—an after supper chat and quiet time. Outside the temperatures had fallen quickly and the wind was bathing the plains with gentle strokes.

All eleven of us were sitting on chairs or on the floor. The stories of life in Kansas were being relived from unimportant events in the school yard to the railroad roundhouse. Nothing out of *our* ordinary life.

In one section of the room my father and two uncles, Tío Esteban and Tío Zacarías occupied the three softest chairs as they always did. They huddled around the A-shaped walnut radio on a table, puffing smoke into the ceiling, and listening intently.

The voice from the radio was strong and confident. FDR, Franklin Delano Roosevelt, our 31st president, was delivering one of his famous "fireside chats." Our country had already plunged in World War II and my father, the leader of our family, was trying to see if he could make any connection to what was happening in Europe and what was occurring in our local area. *New jobs were being posted. But why? Why Pratt?*

I could see clearly the strain on my father's face. Not necessarily a worrisome effort but still one of some concern. I wanted to help but, of course, I didn't know how.

What struck me more than anything else is that for the first time that I can remember, I took notice of the size of my father—in stature, in responsibilities and history.

Compared to my uncles, my father was not a tall man, but taller than most Mexicans at about five-foot-nine. His jet black hair was thinning fast, although we seldom saw it. The sight of my dad was one with a cap over his forehead. I often wondered if he wore it to sleep.

The cap was so much of him that a clear line had formed on his forehead from the blistering summer Kansas sun and the wind-blown winters. His ruddy face, light complexioned, was a visual history of the long years of working in the varied but always hostile Kansas weather. The elements had left their stamp on his face, hands and other parts exposed to the sun and wind.

The muscles on his body, hardened from the toils of the railroad, accentuated his arms and shoulders. He was exceptionally strong, able to easily heft over 200 pounds from the ground to his shoulders. This we know for he often did it lifting a keg of spikes which weighed over 200 pounds to his shoulder to load onto the motorcar or trailer. The strength in his hands was phenomenal. Spike kegs had only a small lip about ¾ of an inch so it was very difficult to hold on to the keg just to move it.

On this particular evening, I noticed for the first time—no reason, just happened to notice then—that his broad shoulders covered the back of the ragged wing chair.

Unlike most adult men of the time, he did not have a mustache. He really didn't need one.

One of ten children from two families, my father came to the United States when some members of the Villarreal family fled the Mexican Revolution[4] from what I hear was a comfortable home and living in Villa del Carmen known locally as "El Chipinque".

It was about 1922 when our family, which consisted only of my father, landed in Chicago. Many other Mexicans, all victims of the revolution, also wound up in the Windy City simply because of the word of mouth that there were jobs and, in a lot of cases, some relatives had preceded them.

By the time my father was a teenager, he joined many other Mexicans and Polish on a railroad that was one of the 48 major railroads serving the Chicago area in that time frame. Of necessity, he learned to speak Polish before English since this was the first language of his co-workers in the Chicago area. Railroad business was still expanding westward. The railroad's expansion and his early experiences eventually brought him to Pratt, Kansas where the Rock Island Railroad (Officially the Chicago Rock Island and Pacific Railroad, CRI&P) had one of its Divisional centers. Initially he was not able to secure a railroad job comparable to what he had in the Chicago area and he worked for a while in the gypsum mines near Sun City south of Pratt.

He was alone, but he had a job, the most important element of survival in a country that was about to be challenged by the Great Depression.

Lucky for my father, other Mexicans already lived in Pratt. Not too many, but enough to share a language and stories of the toils of the railroad.

And two angels, Don Martín and Doña Victoria Blea, came into his life. They took him under their blessed wings in those dreary times by providing a roof and an occasional meal. They also pointed him toward a local young and attractive woman who became my mother. I'll share more about Don Martín and Doña Victoria later.

My father worked on the section gang for the railroad and still managed to have energy left over on weekends. After I started playing baseball in 1947, he started umpiring games some Friday evenings and Saturdays and Sundays during the season.

Some of the stories that my father and uncles shared on those memorable evenings dated back to when he had been a boxer.

"Your dad fought the state champion. I believe it was in 19__," my Tío Zacarías would say, and somehow the year never came.

"It was not a title fight," he would explain and it seemed that he wanted to add that, perhaps that was a blessing in disguise.

No matter how many times Tío Zacarías repeated the story; I always found it fascinating because I waited for more details that never seem to come.

"Okay," Tío Zacarías continued. He then went to say that the match took place one dreadful winter day on a week when a blizzard turned the plains to a sheet of white as far as the eye could see.

Of necessity, my father had piled on the overtime. Good for the paycheck. Not so good for his rest. He had not slept more than a few hours during the whole week.

Needless to say, my father did not win the bout.

"He wasn't knocked out like all the other contenders at that time," Tío Esteban said. "Your dad stood up to him all ten rounds. If it had been any other week, well, your dad might have been the state champ."

As you can see, my dad didn't flinch at many challenges. Except one. Cancer.

The dreadful disease was first detected in 1961 when the pain in his chest was severe enough that he consulted the local M.D. who referred him to a specialist. This called for a nearly 100-mile trip to Halstead for treatment and eventually surgery and radiation, neither of which saved him.

I don't know of many people who have beaten lung cancer since it spreads rather quickly throughout the body. Although he was fighter, he did not win this bout either. We were not really ready to let him go. He was only in his 50s.

GEOGRAPHIC DETAILS

The *barrio* was not large in terms of territory but rich in culture and history. The dimensions were small by today's standards as most neighborhoods or gated communities span several city blocks and include upscale houses. The northern end of the comunidad was approximately the 1400 block of Main Street (US Highway 281) while the southern end would correspond roughly to the 1100 block. The western edge was Main Street where the highway was separated from us by a large steep incline that formed the shoulder of the highway. A path, large enough to drive a car or walk along the highway was below at the same level as the houses that bordered the highway.

The alley divided the western side from the eastern street, Ninnescah which was unpaved as were all other streets that came through the *barrio.* The *barrio* at this time was only about six square blocks but had been larger in the past. During the early years there had been more houses, more residents and other subsections such as the railroad cars furnished by the CRI&P for employees to live in. These were located slightly to the east of the main part where the cars were on railroad property and on the spur track which was gone by the late 30s. There was also a small enclave of four houses that looked more like barracks. These also belonged to the railroad initially but were later sold to families in the area and two were moved out leaving only two that were refurbished and remodeled.

To the southeast of the main residential area was the Roundhouse, a four stall structure that had seen more glorious days in previous years. This structure and the turntable were still in use until around 1957. The majority of diesel locomotive repair operations took place in the "diesel shed" a newer building on the premises. In previous years, the roundhouse had been the focal point of the railroad and of the *barrio* since so many residents had worked there. In the heydays of coal burning steam locomotives a larger labor force worked at the various stages of coal processing and water conditioning. When these old workhorses were replaced with the more modern oil burning locomotives, fewer employees were required for maintenance and even fewer remained when the railroads converted to diesel electric motive power.

The workforce at this time consisted of around 20 men although in past years there had been more repairs performed and more men were employed. Bullgang refers to the laborers who worked on the Rip Track and in and around the Roundhouse. In addition to the Roundhouse, there were other buildings in the area, a washroom/locker room for "bullgang" employees and a better maintained room for engineers and firemen which they used to store their metal trunks that protected their possessions on the locomotive while they were on the road. Any material other than metal would soon have disintegrated due to the heat, metal floor of the locomotive cab and the constant motion sliding a suitcase around.

The "rip track" a section with four tracks was the area where repairs were made to all types of railroad cars from tanks to flatcars. The work here was very heavy and dirty especially when cars need wheels and/or brake beam replacements. These operations also occurred on a siding where a car had been cut out of a train and sometimes was on the ground when the journal had broken and the wheel had come off. One other large building called the "mill" was the site where boxcars were repaired and there was adequate machinery to construct wooden replacements for worn out or broken sections as well as welding equipment for fixing metal parts.

During WWII in the area close to the roundhouse, with a spur track connecting it to the main line, there was a fenced, guarded area with a series of tanks which the military had installed to store fuel for the airbase. This small area had a guard on duty 24 hours a day and each guard had his own dog to assist in discouraging would be intruders. This facility was built on the *barrio* side of the railroad property and had ready access to the highway so that tank trucks could haul fuel to the airbase.

The other accessories to these railroad buildings were the sand house and the water and oil cranes where laborers equipped locomotives with necessary supplies such as sand, water and fuel. These same laborers performed similar operations on locomotives at the depot while the train was stopped to discharge and take on passengers, drop off mail and baggage and supply the dining car and coaches with ice, water and other supplies.

This whole area was within walking distance from all houses and for all employees who lived in the *barrio* although the older employees took a little longer to get to and from work.

In the more remote past there had been a spur track closer to the main part of the *barrio* where several families lived. The housing had been provided by the railroad and increased the population by 20 or more persons.

THE VILLARREAL COMPOUND

At first glance, our family compound was a mixture of old lumber that generally made up four walls topped with asphalt roofs. I call it a compound because it involved a series of structures, and lots of family. Togetherness was a way of life.

There were eleven of us at one time or another.

Aside from my parents, my sister, my brother and me, the extended family also included my maternal grandmother, Doña María Palacios de Maldonado, born 8/15/1885 died 10/30/1960, a grandaunt, Tía Preciliana Palacios de Chabolla and her husband, Tío Zacarías, she, born 1/4/1876 died 8/27/1960, he, born 1878 died 1946; two uncles, Tío Emilio born 6/10/1905 died 12/13/1994, and Tío Epifanio born11/10/1915, died 3/28/1997, both Maldonados; and one grand uncle, Tío Esteban Palacios, born 6/3/1881, died 12/31/1970.

This means that in our particular household there were *only* three generations, I say

only because in the barrio, there were households with fewer or an equal number of generations but more people. There were many times in the *barrio* when I simply lost track of who lived where and with whom.

The main house consisted of six rooms, including a kitchen and a living room and *no bathrooms*. Our bathrooms were really *restrooms,* if you could rest in a closet that was hot in the summer and freezing on most days of the winter. We had two such closets, one of these was special. It was a *two-holer*; meaning two people could do their business at the same time, which happened only in dire emergencies like bad cases of diarrhea.

Eight of us lived in the main house, the five of us that included my father, my mother, my sister, my brother and my grandmother, Doña María and Tío Zacarías and Tía Preciliana. The main house was originally two separate dwellings together but not connected. In later years the gap between the two was sealed up and the two became one, a larger one. My immediate family installed a kitchen in the northeast room and divided the remaining space into a livingroom/bedroom/sittingroom and two other bedrooms. The grandparents kept the southern rooms of the original house which still had the kitchen with the woodburning stove. My family opted for a more modern electric range. (Note: We did have electricity, even isolated farms had that, but we had no other modern utilities yet.)

The house was not weather tight and the morning following blizzard nights we awoke to small snowdrifts beside the doors where the snow had blown in under the door and through the keyhole. The windows were frosted on the inside periodically during the cold season and what little moisture was inside the house ended up as frost on the windows. Our weatherproofing consisted mainly of stuffing newspaper into the cracks around the doors and windows. This helped some but the wind is tenacious and finds a way to slither in through the tiniest opening. The later version of weatherproofing consisted of plastic sheets nailed to the screen doors and window openings.

During the dustbowl days, fine sand particles came through the miniscule gaps that now allowed the fine snow to penetrate the living space. Kansas seemed to always have some airborne element stalking the population. At least with snow, persons did not have to cover their face with a damp cloth like they had to with the dust from the blowing sand in previous years. Fortunately for us the dustbowl days were over but there were still thunderstorms that blew dust into the house.

The family home was definitely not soundproof either as we always heard the wind howling in all seasons but it was more threatening when it blew the snow across the wheat fields to the north of us. Many times we woke up to snowdrifts several feet high next to the house, sometimes blocking the door but mostly on the north side of the house and the garage on the northwest corner of the property.

Some 20 feet south of the main house was another small house. This one belonged to Tío Esteban. It consisted of two rooms, both with outside entrances. The door connecting the two rooms was closed most of the year. Tío Esteban lived in the east room with a heating stove, a bed, a wardrobe and a chair. I don't remember if there was any other furniture. We respected his privacy and did not enter unless personally invited.

The west room, not to be confused with the "West Wing" of recent TV fame on NBC, was not heated during the cold months of the year. My two younger uncles, Tío Emilio and Tío Epifanio slept in this room and had a wardrobe and little else.

One of my occasional chores in those days was to wake up my uncles. Most of the time, their room was open and they didn't mind if we wandered in. On many winter mornings, I found water, kept by the bed for a nighttime drink, frozen. Occasionally, I noticed that other liquids in the room were also frozen, but I won't dwell on this.

Both uncles were hardy persons and seemed to thrive on sleeping in a very cold room. And then again, maybe not—they went to bed with heavy quilts and raccoon coats piled on top to keep them warm.

TWO GARAGES LIKE BOOKENDS

There were few automobiles in this country in the 1940s and very few of them found their way to our *barrio*. One of them was ours, a very used, previously owned nondescript car with many miles and sunburned paint.

So let's start with the garage. Yes, we had a garage, actually two. One of them was on the northwest corner, which housed the car. Needless to add, we were not a two-car family for many years.

In front of the garage was a small sturdy shed about 6' by 5' with slats in the doorway. The shed had a metal covering on the roof and a small door in the roof that latched from the inside with a metal bar. The door in the roof was for the coal delivery truck to dump the coal into the shed. The slats in the doorway were to keep the coal from falling out of front door of the shed.

When we hauled coal into the house, we had to get the coal from the top of the pile in this shed out through the front door. Usually we had to break up the large pieces in order to haul them in the metal bucket into the house. We used some of the larger pieces for banking the stoves at night and a large piece would usually burn all night and keep a room fairly warm.

Now, let me get to the second garage. The two garages, one at each end, diagonally opposite each other, were like bookends on our two lots. These garages were merely shells with large doors for a car to enter but had no insulation. To say these garages were cold in the winter would be an understatement.

Next to the northwest garage on its south side were the two outhouses. Aside from the classic "two holer," there was a more sanitary outhouse approved and built to city specifications by city employees as part of the civic improvement program in impoverished city areas.

OF TOOLS AND SHEDS

Surrounding the compound was high fence, a wire fence probably ordered from one of the catalogs and installed by the men in the family. A short distance to the south, just past the sidewalk leading to the west gate, there were two storage sheds. One belonged to Tío Zacarías. This was a tool shed where he kept many different types of tools and all of his gardening equipment and supplies.

I was always attracted to a shelf, where kept several books in a small room within this shed. He kept the outside door locked with a padlock and the inner room locked with a lock in the door, to which, only he had a key.

Occasionally we got a look inside but it was not a public area even for family members. I recall that there were poetry books, volumes of classic novels and other useful books, all in Spanish.

Tío Zacarías read quite a bit and his newspaper of choice was *La Prensa*[5], a Spanish language weekly, which arrived by mail from San Antonio, Texas.

Two benches with an interesting feature were in the front of the building. There we sat and read on many summer evenings. The interesting feature of the benches was that they had old caboose cushions that were heavy cloth and stuffed with excelsior and horsehair. This was long before the use of foam rubber filling for cushions. The cushions were from the cupola of the old wooden caboose.

To the south of this building, was another shed that contained assorted junk stored out of the way. The distance between these two sheds was about ten feet.—not much room but enough to serve as a playground for the adventurous youth to jump from the roof of one to the other. The jump could only be made from the north to the south as the roof was slanted up toward the south and the extra height would allow a soaring jump toward the south shed. The roof on the south shed was also slanted toward the south so the landing area was compatible with a daring jump. The north shed roof was long enough to gather a little speed for the jump.

To the south of this shed was a lumber pile where boards of unknown origin and decaying condition lay untouched for many years. There was an old carpenter's bench with a vise amidst the woodpile. The carpenter's table was weather-beaten and falling apart. The vise was somewhat rusted but useable. In later years, after Tío Zacarías died, the old lumber was cut up for firewood. I salvaged the vise, a treasure still in use in my work area. In between this shed and the main house was open space where both granduncles had gardens.

AND EVEN A CABOOSE

An old caboose adorned the west end of the main house. It was not unusual to see cabooses and other freight cars in the neighborhoods in those days.

Our caboose served to store firewood, dried chiles (*ristras*), household items, and sports equipment. It also doubled as an adventure theater where we could escape into a make believe land and travel the world viewing it from the cupola of the caboose.

In really cold weather it served as a refrigerator and freezer for short-term storage. Immediately next to the caboose and slightly west of the main house was a storm cellar where other items were stored such as potatoes, jars of chiles and other preserved items. It served its other intended purpose, that of shelter during the many thunderstorms and tornadoes in the summer. Those of us at home, young children and adult females, sought and found shelter here on numerous summer afternoons and read by the light of a kerosene lamp, a more modern one than the old whale oil lamps. The roof of the cellar served as a drying surface for the yams that my granduncle cultivated as well as for drying, anything else in the sun. We didn't dry clothes there since there was perfectly useable and modern clothesline in the yard which consisted of three wires strung between two poles about 15 feet apart. There was usually a small pole propping up the middle of these lines to support the weight of wet clothes.

PETS AND VARMINTS

A pig, chickens and dogs were also part of my upbringing. These animals lived in several buildings west of the caboose. These buildings, while strong and sturdy at some time, eventually were torn down after we sold the pig and either ate or sold the chickens. On occasions we had doghouses on this part of the compound.

I remember that many, many years ago, probably around 1941, rats invaded the foundation of Tío Esteban's house. No problem if you had a 22 caliber rifle.

On many occasions Tío Zacarías would sit at a window in the main house with his .22 caliber rifle and shoot rats as they emerged from under the house. He could do this on moonlit nights when the rats came out and were visible. They probably ventured out on dark nights too but no one could see them and certainly not well enough to shoot them. Finally after many rats had fallen to the 22, there weren't any left and the foundation was cleaned up.

We poured concrete around the house, which served two purposes: strengthening the foundation and keeping any other vermin from invading. We still got mice that migrated from the wheat fields and other areas close to the house but we usually trapped the ones that got into the house and did not bother the ones that got into the woodpile or outbuildings. Neighborhood cats, including ours, patrolled these areas and properly disposed of the mice.

Moles were a different type of varmint that messed up the garden and other areas where they tunneled. In the garden it was easy to follow their progress as they raised the earth a little as they traveled in their tunnels.

We used a metal contraption to get rid of the moles. It consisted of a long handle, a set of prongs that straddled the tunnel and a spiked prong that could cut off the progress of the mole through the ground. There are two of these contraptions in my possession now which might be considered collectibles if one were inclined to collect this type of mechanism.

Moles were never a major problem but they did eat the roots of plants and the plants died as a result. This was not serious for most plants but for the *chile* plants, it was very serious. Thanks, in part to our contraption, we got rid of moles and, more importantly, saved the *chile* harvest.

EL MOLINO DE VIENTO[6]

We had the most popular windmill in the *barrio*.

Our windmill not only provided water for the family but also for the gardens of my granduncles and for workers in the wheat fields nearby.

Those who combined the wheat were called harvest hands. Persons who worked on farms were commonly called farm hands so the term "hand" also applied to other jobs. For example, mill hands would be persons who worked in the mills, section hands, like my father, were persons who worked on the section gang on the railroad.

Every summer custom cutters came to harvest the wheat with their combines and large trucks. These crews started their custom cutting in Texas and followed the ripening of the wheat north. They came through Oklahoma, Kansas, on up through the other states and ended up in Canada.

While they were working in the area, they came to our house to fill their containers with cool, clear water from our well. The windmill was a sort of landmark for the crews who had come through before, and they all knew that the water there was good.

The windmill ran almost continuously throughout the spring and summer with the aid of gentle winds. Come winter, the winds were gone, so we pumped water by hand. Winter winds usually accompanied snow or cold and we only needed water for household use during this time of year. Some times, we pumped water in the spring or summer if there was not enough wind to run the windmill.

There are some chores that boys just leave to their dads. Maintaining the windmill was one of those.

Maintenance on the windmill consisted of changing the oil in the gearbox behind the wheel that converted wind energy to reciprocal motion driving the pumping mechanism, which drew water. My father usually performed this delicate operation which required climbing the steel tower, then draining the old oil and filling the gearbox with new oil.

I hated heights so I never climbed to the top to work on the mechanism. I performed other work that did not require climbing.

The well itself had a pipe, which connected the water table to the surface, a pipe approximately two-and-a-half inches in diameter. Within this pipe there was a sandpoint at the bottom of the well that filtered the water that came up through the pipe.

The sandpoint was replaced only once that I can remember and a plumber with a special tool snagged the old one and brought it to the surface. We had noticed for a couple of months that the water was getting a little brownish in color and that small sand particles were getting to the surface. The diagnosis of a corroded sandpoint was correct as the new one cleared the water.

The previous sandpoint was the original one that had gone into the well when it was first drilled and the windmill was installed about 20 years previous. In order to remove the old sandpoint, it was necessary to pull the pump rods and bring up the valve from the bottom of the well like we did periodically when changing the pump leathers.

I assisted in this latter operation, as I grew older and stronger. In order to pull the rods, which were wooden and therefore slippery and wet, we had to remove the top parts of the pump itself.

First we had to shut down the windmill and secure the control arm so that it would not inadvertently start pumping. The next step was to tie the top part of the pumping mechanism to one side after disconnecting it from the pump rod. This top rod connected the gearbox on the top of the windmill to the steel rod on the top of the pump. Once we had this rod tied off to the side, we unscrewed the top part of the pump, a circular metal top. We then unscrewed the pump rod from the first wooden rod.

In order to pull the slippery rods, it was necessary to grip them securely either by hand or by some other means. We always used the other means due to the weight of the rods and the difficulty in pulling them out. We secured a length of chain around the wooden rod and with a strong metal rod, or sometimes a 2-by-4 piece of lumber, and then looped through this chain. Once we completed this step, we started pulling the wooden rods out of the well.

At each joint, approximately 20 feet, we had to unscrew the rod from the string below.

There were nine or ten long wooden rods and one short one at the bottom that was connected to the valve. Once all the rods were out, we dismantled the valve and installed new pump leathers. These leathers provided a seal at the bottom of the pipe that enabled the pump to raise the water from the bottom to the spigot at the top.

Pump leathers were actually made of leather and shaped like a thin concave doughnut.

The pump leathers effectively closed the pipe so that water would not leak down around the valve but rather would fill the pipe and lift toward the surface. The pump leathers were placed with the hollow part facing toward the middle of the valve mechanism.

Leathers usually lasted two or three years but in years when it was very hot in the summer, the windmill pumped more and wore out the leathers in one year, sometimes in just one summer.

The valve was simply a one way door that allowed water to pass up into the pipe as the rod went down. As the rod came up, the valve closed and water was lifted. On the flowing stroke, the rod went down and the valve opened allowing water to fill the space created by the valve and the pipe. Each stroke lifted water higher until it reached the surface, at which time the water continued to run as long as someone was pumping or the windmill was turning.

The last part of this operation was the reassembling of the pump. After the valve portion had gone in first and all the other rods had been connected, we reassembled the pump mechanism and reconnected the windmill rod

We then turned on the windmill. If there was no wind, we pumped by hand for a few minutes. If the water ran discolored at first, it soon cleared up.

Putting the rods back was much easier than pulling them out as gravity helped. This part of the job was still delicate since a slip of a rod would result in the loss of the parts remaining in the well and would have necessitated the help of a well driller or someone who could operate a "fishing tool." Note: An oil well operates on the same principle as the water well but is much larger and deeper and the parts are heavier.

Fortunately for us, we never had a misstep in doing this job. A large pipe wrench held the rod column from slipping back into the well uncontrolled. I haven't any idea what happened to that large wrench which today might be a collector's item.

Prior to World War II, one or more of my uncles had helped my father in this operation but when they went to war, only my granduncles were left to help. When I was older and strong enough to handle the job, I became the prime helper and only my father and I performed this duty.

The windmill was sold sometime after I left the *barrio* and I do not know who bought it or where it went. Other wells in the barrio pumped good water for a time but since the owners did not change the pump leathers on any regular basis; their water supply was not as plentiful, clear or as tasty as ours.

One other job during the winter was to drain the top part of the pump so that it did not freeze and burst. There was a small cavity under the pump about four-feet deep where the pump mechanism connected to the actual well pipe. There was a petcock, a small drain valve, which one of us was assigned to open on nights when the temperature was predicted to fall below freezing.

Had we not done this, the pump could have frozen and broken. The force of water freezing and expanding could easily break the metal pump, which was made of cast iron, which is somewhat brittle.

I almost always got this assignment and fortunately for the pump and me I did not forget to do it.

The pump had ruptured on one-occasion years before when the large valve feeding the hose to the garden was closed and the front valve was also closed. As the windmill was turned on in a high wind, the water coming up had no place to go due to the closed valves, so it took a course of its own through the side of the pump housing.

The pump had filled up quickly and finally burst through a side from the pressure of the water. After we repaired the pump, it worked fine as before but carried a bronze scar on the side where it had cracked and then been welded.

During the real hot summers, the windmill ran almost non-stop. We tended the watering of the garden even after it was dark and harder to see. When we watered one or more of us moved the hose from one furrow to another.

It took about fifteen minutes to fill one furrow. The garden had close to 40 furrows so it took a long time to water the garden and we napped in between the moving of the hose. Hot summers were right for sleeping outdoors anyway so this night duty was not truly bad since it was much cooler outdoors than indoors. This was not an all night job, only until around 10 p.m. or when the wind died.

Other times we watered early in the morning, around 5 o'clock and late in the afternoon. The amount of water needed depended on how hot the day became and the season. Early spring required more watering to help the plants grow. Later on they did not need as much water and in the fall, they needed less as they were now mature and yielding vegetables--and most important of all, green *chiles*.

THE MIGHTY HONEY LOCUST

For many years a tall spry Honey Locust sat in the center of Tío Esteban's portion of the garden. The grand Honey Locust shaded a great portion of the garden. We enjoyed resting in its shade or lounging around in the furrows of the sweet potatoes that grew on his side of the yard.

This was one of a few cool places available during the late summer. The furrows were about a foot high, which means that there was a sort of canyon in between the furrows. For small kids, it was deep enough to lie in and be almost totally covered by the vines. If we had not watered that part of the garden on a particular day, the furrows were dry but cool and very pleasant to lie in.

A word about sweet potatoes: These Yams provided a fall activity that lasted for weeks. First we cut off the vines which by this time had started to die and dry out. Then we dug up the yams with a potato fork. At that time I did not know what it was called. After digging up the yams, it was necessary to properly age them. We did this by spreading them on top of the storm cellar, a cement surface that absorbed the heat of the sun. Every morning we, usually one of us young kids spread them in the sun and left them there all day and retrieved them at night. The yams rested overnight in baskets eagerly awaiting their sunbathing which would begin again in the morning.

For many years this was an annual experience. Finally when Tío Zacarías died, so did the cultivation of yams.

One day in late August in the mid 1940s, Tío Esteban announced:

"That tree has got to go."

My brother, a young child at the time, and I just looked at each other rather stunned.

The reason he gave was that the roots were adversely affecting the rest of the garden by absorbing most of the water.

Honey Locusts are fairly hard and not easy to chop down.

Early the next morning after this pronouncement, he started preparations for chopping down the tree. The axe he used was an old double-bitted one that was sharp but not much of a match for the hard trunk of the tree. After toiling for a couple of hours and not finishing the job, he took a long rest. By then it was hotter, remember August in Kansas is not yet fall and although the nights have begun to cool down a tiny bit the days are still very hot.

Finally after procrastinating most of the day, he attacked the tree around 5 p.m. when it had begun to cool down. For an hour or more Tío Esteban slammed the trunk of the tree until darkness and tiredness finally ended his day.

Then, as he was just about to quit for the day, he decided to give it one more whack. A smile filled his round, sweaty face: the tree was ready to topple.

We waited in vain for one more whack of the ax but Tío Esteban placed the ax by the tree and walked back to his house anyway it was Suppertime.

The next morning we arose early, as was our custom, and could hardly wait to see the mighty tree on the ground. But the battle was still not over.

We tied a rope to the highest part that we could reach and stretched the rope to a safe distance in the direction we wanted the tree to fall. Tío Esteban chopped the final portion holding the tree as several of us pulled the rope toward us anticipating a successful climax to our tree job.

Despite our hefty pull in one direction, the tree toppled in another direction pulling all of us to the side that gravity took it.

The mess it made was not colossal but it took another half day to clean up the branches, wood chips and broken plants.

It would be a year later before the Honey Locust would be through with us. We still had to dig out the tree's roots from the garden.

The roots were more difficult to deal with than the tree's trunk. By then I was a year older and stronger and could chop with the heavy axe. In a matter of two and one half days, we were able to clear out the rest of the tree that we had killed the previous year. Gone was the shade the tree had provided but the garden seemed to thrive without it.

The death of the mighty Honey Locust also set in motion a series of events that pretty much put an end to our gardening. First, World War II had taken my two young uncles to Europe and the South Pacific. When they returned they got married and set up their own households—and their own gardens on a very much smaller scale.

My father was always too busy with his duties on the section gang and building chores to devote any time to gardening.

Tío Emilio continued to garden at his own house, but then he was transferred when the railroad moved its main operations out of our town in the late 1950s. Commuting took a lot of time and he could only come home on weekends.

The many chores around the house kept him busy and left little time for gardening. In later years after he retired from the railroad, he again tended a larger garden. His specialty was hot *chiles*[7], which he ate fresh. He preserved many in different ways and strung *ristras* [8]with the red, mature ones.

His special *ristras* were his seed stock from which he selected the best of the best and planted the seed for the next and ensuing years. Tío Zacarías had selected the best *chiles* from seed from previous years and the varieties that my uncle and the other *barrio* gardeners used were primarily those that he had carefully cultivated and developed.

CEMENT BLOCKS

During my high school years one of my major chores was making cement blocks. This was a daily event in good weather and included watering the blocks daily for the first two weeks and periodically thereafter, to ensure proper curing.

My father had bought a small machine to make blocks, which he used whenever he had a moment to spare, usually weekends. I made blocks after school and on weekends. While I call it a machine, it was actually a jig that held a wooden pallet and had metal cylinders that formed the holes in the blocks. It was strictly manual labor even though my brother Manuel did not participate in this recreation.

All the work of mixing the cement, packing the cement into the mold, removing the block from the mold (very carefully), and placing the block on the ground close to the work are manual operations. Absent a real machine that could perform all the functions necessary for making blocks, this was the only way that we could produce cement blocks economically.

After more than three years of toil we had enough blocks to start construction of a house on two lots that my father had purchased years earlier. During this period I had used a couple of the blocks as barbell weights. One block on each end of an iron bar was heavy enough to give me a good workout doing several lifts.

He designed the house and built it over a period of a year and a few months. The house was not totally finished until after I had moved to another town to work prior to my reporting date for Navy flight training. My family moved into the new house while I was in the Navy so I did not get to move in until later. My family enjoyed the house with city amenities such as indoor plumbing and unlimited hot water.

I did not live in this house full time as I went to the University of Kansas after leaving the Navy and spent little time in this house except during school vacations. This new house had no garage detached or otherwise but did have a parking area to one side and on street parking in front.

The timbers for the new house had been salvaged from the wooden caboose on the old house property. The house had a hip roof, which we covered with asphalt shingles. Since I hate heights and had to put on the asphalt roofing it was noteworthy that I managed to finish it in one weekend without hanging on to something thus hampering my work or falling off.

This house was many steps up from our old house which had started out as two smaller buildings with a small gap between the two. In later years the gap was boarded up and the two became one, the main house but it was not comparable to the new house which was much more modern.

Tío Esteban moved into the big house during World War II after my two younger uncles, Tío Emilio and Tío Epifanio, went into the army. He had rented his house to a couple from San Antonio Texas while they were stationed at the airbase.

BEGINNING OF FORMAL EDUCATION

Kindergarten was a shocking experience for me. I remember that I got to school and learned that only English was being spoken—by the teacher, of course, and by white and colored classmates who answered simple questions which I did not understand and so could not answer. As I previously mentioned, my mother, two uncles and my father all spoke English at work but they did not do so at home. My mother did the shopping and ran other errands in the English speaking community. My father had to speak English, along with phrases in other languages when he made work assignments to the rest of the section gang. He served as foreman most of the year but was not paid the regular foreman wage since the assignment was considered temporary. My two younger uncles were high school graduates and worked at the roundhouse where English was the language of communication. None of these folks had taught me English prior to my adventures in kindergarten.

I understood a word here and there that I had picked up from our play time, but for the most part, I was lost.

I adapted very fast to what would now be called "Academic English".

My memories are somewhat muddled regarding the rest of my kindergarten year but I did increase my vocabulary beyond the few survival words that I picked up on the playground and in the halls. The academic work in Kindergarten at that time was not really heavy, nor involved. Sandbox and playground require little vocabulary or communication for that matter.

And I still remember that in grade school the nuns didn't allow the boys and the girls to play together. In the primary grades the girls played in the playhouse and the boys played with the blocks in rainy weather or on a small portion of the playground the rest of the time. All others played on the bare playground or on the portions covered with vegetation, sandburrs, stickers that hurt as much in pulling them out as they did when they went into our skin.

Somehow I survived kindergarten and was set for academic life. I remember very little about first grade but I must have learned to read fairly well. How else can I explain my promotions from the "little room", grades 1-2-3, to the "middle room", grades 4-5-6, to the "big room", grades 7-8, as the Catholic School was divided.

Religion consumed my early learning. Much of the early reading was on Bible stories. Spelling lists were filled with ecclesiastical terms rather than everyday words in common usage. These were words that no one ever used in conversation and I never read them anywhere in the readings that we were assigned.

The school library consisted of a few books but none of any particular interest. I learned little by serving as an *altar boy*.[9] The language consisted of the Latin mass responses and to this day I have only a slight clue of what we knew by memory and recited daily.

The town's newspaper did provide some extra reading. I loved reading comic books but the nuns took care of this vice quickly. Anyone caught trying to read comic books in class or even on school grounds got a ruler slammed on their knuckles.

During my eight years at Sacred Heart Catholic School, I attended class in a multi- grade classroom. Always an avid reader, this gave me a challenging opportunity to read with students in higher grades and do math above grade level. It challenged all of us to work harder but we learned more than by staying at or below grade level.

I learned quickly to appreciate the sound teachings of the nuns when I attended public schools for the first time as a freshman in high school. To my surprise, I was elected representative from my freshman homeroom to the student council.

Even more amazing—at least to me--I was then elected junior class president, a first for anyone of Mexican descent.

A SHOESHINE STAND

One summer when I was ten or eleven, I decided to try a business. I asked a neighbor to join me to set up a shoeshine stand.

The idea of a shoeshine stand was just one mistake. The bigger mistake was that our *barrio* had no paved streets and alleys worse than the streets.

Next mistake was opting for a shady spot between two outbuildings in our back yard. It just did not occur to us at the time that people, who walk around on dirt, mud and loose sand would not be much interested in getting their shoes shined on a daily or even infrequent basis.

The result was that the volume of foot traffic at our end of the barrio was about two pedestrians per day on busy days.

After three days, we still had no customers.

We took turns tending the stand. While my business partner went home to eat, I was the manager. While I went to eat, my partner was the manager. While we were both there, no one was the manager as there was no business anyway and we played checkers.

After a week of non-activity, we concluded that this business was not very good. The week's adventure in the shoeshine business resulted in a business loss of about $1.25. We determined then that our next business venture would be in an area that had a better chance at more profit. There was not much opportunity for business ventures in the *barrio*.

SO WE TRIED CONSTRUCTION

By the time I was a teenager, I was at an awkward age—big and strong, even for my age, but not old enough to be in the labor force. I still managed to get a construction job, where the pay was not bad, every now and then.

On one occasion six of us in the *barrio* were hired for the weekend to set forms for concrete on a bridge about seven miles from town.

It was in the fall of the year and cold weather had set in making the work harder and more dangerous. We were to pour concrete the next day and it was getting colder by the time we finished setting the forms in the afternoon.

When we arrived at the bridge site the next day, I noticed that Satch, one of my coworkers from the *barrio,* was wearing three or four old raggedy sport coats to keep warm. The rest of us had sweatshirts and overalls over long underwear and were fairly comfortable.

Satch, who had dropped out of school in the third or fourth grade, had safety pins holding the front of his sport coats together but the pins kept bending and releasing and exposing him to the cold wind. To protect himself from howling wind, Satch chose to run the concrete mixer, a choice assignment and warmer job.

The rest of us either shoveled sand, cement and gravel for the mixer or hauled concrete in wheelbarrows from the mixer to the bridge and poured it into the forms. Luckily, we finished the job around 3 p.m. Satch, my friend and buddy, was a good example of the times and the poverty that forced us to do with second hand clothing and hand-me downs.

THE WEDDING

Life, for the most part, was dull in the *barrio,* especially if you were a teenager. So when our parents informed us of an out of town trip and a wedding to boot, we looked forward to it—with mixed emotions.

This particular trip took us about three hours away by car but we had to dress up, which we didn't really mind. The Kansas plain countryside didn't offer much excitement, but hearing our parents chat about the bride and the groom and their parents provided an interesting conversation and traveling entertainment.

In those days, women were considered old maids if they were not married by their late teens. This bride to be was already in her 20s.

The conversation went something like this:

"I don't know why she waited so long to get married. She is very pretty."

"She was probably just waiting for my *compadre's* [10]young son to be ready for marriage."

Once we got to the wedding celebration, the fun started quickly. We got to see relatives whose names didn't come to mind easily and made friendships that generally would last for the duration of the event.

Getting through the Catholic ceremony, which always involved a rather long Mass, was tedious at best. But then came the real fun. Food and a dance awaited us.

It was customary for the groom's family to pay for the wedding but the bride's mother was widely known as a good cook. The groom's mother was not a semi-famous cook, so the bride's family prepared the meal.

There were many guests attending from out of town and the food was served buffet style with a very long line. The food consisted of the usual wedding fare, chicken, fried, barbecued, and *mole* (not the English word for a rodent but a Mexican dish made with red chile). In addition there were refried beans, rice, vegetables of several varieties, tamales, green chile with pork and hot tortillas rolled by one of the bride's four younger sisters.

Our family was just about at the end of the serving line. My younger brother was behind me and there were only a couple of people behind us. Someone cracked a joke. We broke out laughing uncontrollably.

As we continued through the serving line, my brother was still laughing when he slobbered a little into the mashed potatoes. Not knowing what exactly to do, he did the only sensible thing, he stirred the potatoes.

Since we had both already served ourselves mashed potatoes, it didn't bother us much. No one else noticed and since we were still laughing, others presumed that we were still chuckling at the joke. In any case there was only a small portion of mashed potatoes left and the serving dish was removed before we sat down to eat.

Needless to say, we did not go back for seconds on those potatoes. A couple of others did go back for seconds but suffered no ill effects probably because there was a new batch of "unslobbered" potatoes.

The next event was the dance which started around 4 p.m. and, finally ended around midnight. The father of the bride was an excellent musician renowned for his mandolin playing, violin playing and guitar virtuosity. The oldest son was also a good string player and the two of them started the dance with a nice waltz for the bride and groom neither of whom was a great dancer.

After a few more dances my dad joined them on guitar for the next several pieces and was replaced later by other local string players. There used to be a lot of talented string players in those days so it was not difficult to trade off and give other musicians a rest. Most of the "barrio" musicians played guitar or mandolin largely because these were readily available and more moderately priced than pianos or even violins. A person could be self taught on guitar but not usually on violin. Pianos were too heavy to carry around to various functions and were expensive to buy and to keep in tune. Further with more than one generation in most homes there was no room for a piano until and unless the house was expanded and the occupants could afford an inexpensive one.

Oh, one more thing.

The groom, a rather shy one, had made it known that he didn't want his car to be decorated. He carefully hid his car away from the community center where the reception was held.

At about eleven that night, the groom went to get his car. It was not there.

Several of us watched laughing as he went from car to car. Finally, one of his relatives, who obviously had an extra key, came out and directed him to his car.

But when the groom went to open the door, his hands kept slipping. The jokers had greased the driver's door handle.

We had a good laugh and eventually so did the groom, especially after the bride joined him on the way to their honeymoon.

WHAT, NO TELEVISION?

I grew up in an age where there was no television.

Yes, no television. And no computers, no video games and no picture cellular telephones.

What we did have in our home and in the *barrio* were storytellers. They were great at telling us stories that always kept our interest and our imaginations sharp.

We were glad to have storytellers in our family for evening entertainment especially during the shorter days when it was dark by the time we finished our chores. After our evening meal and after the clearing of the table and washing and drying the dishes, we enjoyed story telling.

Many nights, snowy or otherwise, the old folks told us stories around the kitchen table before we went to bed. Friday nights we stayed up a little bit later since there were no classes on Saturday.

Some of these stories dealt with buried treasures and persons who found them but didn't take anything home. The main point of most of these was that the finder later committed suicide or died in some other way after discovering the treasure but not taking anything from it and thereby losing all of it.

The storytellers were always the older folks, grandma, grandaunt, grand uncles and sometimes my dad.

The stories that granduncles and other old folks told dealt with hidden treasures in the mountains in Chihuahua, México and other interesting topics. I think that many of these stories were urban legends long before there were urban legends in the U S. The legend of *La Llorona*[11], for example, is a very old one and familiar in most of the New World. The stories were a type of story that had a moral for children. Other stories were traditional ones that the old folks must have heard from their grandparents.

The stories may have had a religious overtone but we did not recognize it at the time. For example, there were stories about disobedient children who were abducted by the devil. These stories evoked the same type of reaction that flying saucer tales do today. *Entierros*, that is, buried treasures were much like the UFOs of the last century.

Many of these stories included some mysterious light that seemed to mark the place where a treasure was buried and that helped the lonely traveler to spot the treasure. This is reminiscent of the pot of gold at the end of the rainbow.

When the old folks lived in Chihuahua Mexico there probably were many treasures buried in various remote mountain places. During the time of revolutions and other disasters, people tend to hoard what they have and that includes money, jewels and objects of value. Oftentimes people did hide treasures to keep them from the invaders of their town or to otherwise keep their money safe.

When occupants of villages died or were killed by bandits or other robbers, their treasures remained hidden. It is entirely possible that there are still many treasures hidden in the mountains of Mexico and the southwestern U.S.

The moral, if any, of the *entierro* stories was that the person who found the treasure but didn't take advantage received a rope from the person that he told about the treasure. I say "he" since none of these stories involved a female finding a treasure.

The instructions to the finder were to hang himself with the rope provided. The twisted moral may be that if you do not take advantage of an opportunity, you deserve to die. Given the poverty that the old folks experienced, this may have been more relevant to their childhood and that notion pushed them to take advantage of opportunity in whatever form it arrived.

There were funny stories about kids that played practical jokes on people and were later punished either on earth or by the devil.

Other stories simply dealt with an apparition of the devil in disguise. One example was that of some bad kids in the village where my maternal grandparents lived in Chihuahua. There were some kids who were, allegedly, nasty to everyone, talked back to their elders and were generally misbehaving on a regular basis. One day, as the story goes, there was a donkey at the outskirts of the village and one of the bad kids decided to ride it. He got on the donkey and beckoned to his friends to join him. As more and more kids got on, there still was room on the donkey's back.

When all the bad kids had mounted the donkey, which had grown larger to accommodate them all, it flew off with them. The residents insisted that the devil had taken them because they were so bad. No one in the village was sad to see them go. Sounded kind of like the Pied Piper story from another culture.

My sister insists that the version she remembers of this particular story involved a horse rather than a donkey. Since the story took place in Mexico, the donkey is more likely to be the bearer of bad kids.

One story that my father told about his village in Mexico was about witchcraft. According to his story, there was an elderly woman who had strange powers and did unexplainable things. According to my father, this older woman in his village once drew her finger across the top of a bucket full of water and the mark that she made on the surface, stayed on the water until someone finally poured the water out. He said that this happened when he was very young.

Mexican boys did not play Cowboys but rather *Charro,* the forerunner of the North American Cowboy. Playing *Charro* could sometimes be dangerous in the old days.

In this country, this would have been like playing Cowboy, or Cowboys and Indians, a western pastime. There were *Charros* before there were Cowboys since this and many other ideas and events actually came to the Southwest United States from Mexico.

In one event that my father told us about, it seems that one of my father's older brothers was on a small cliff and another brother was running like a wild steer and his brother was trying to lasso him. My dad was only a spectator, or at least this is what he said.

The brother running was almost out of range when his older brother threw the *riata* and the rope caught him around the neck. As he fell off the cliff, the rope tightened around his neck. He dangled for a few seconds until the other brothers picked him up and loosened the rope around his neck and removed it.

Fortunately, no one was seriously hurt but they all were worried for a while that one of the brothers had come close to being killed. The *Charro* game was a little tamer for a week. The younger brother had a rope burn on his neck for several days after the adventure.

Along with the stories at home we learned poesías, short poems. The poems that we learned were very short but many families recited similar *poesías* and had the kids learn them at an early age.

For example, the following included pointing to the east then to the west to show the rising and setting of the sun.

"Aquí sale el sol, y aquí se mete. Y cuando llueve, hay mucho zoquete." The translation to English would lose all the meaning and if it rhymed, it would not make much sense.

One particular recitation of a poem caused my parents embarrassment and, likely a chuckle afterwards. This particular poem was also a point and click performance with the motions of up and down and towards the corner of the room. It makes no sense in translation to English but was a good performing opportunity for small children. The poem went as follows: **"Aquí está la luna comiendo su tuna, tirando las**

cáscaras a la laguna. Allí está el sol comiendo requesón, tirando el saco al mero rincón." On this particular occasion the parish priest was visiting and sitting in the chair close to the corner of the room and it altered the poem due to his position in the room. The poem came out as **"Aquí está la luna comiendo su tuna. Aquí esta el sol comiendo requesón, tirando el saco al mero padre**." Since the good father did not understand Spanish, he merely acknowledged the recitation without comment about the content. All who were present of our family snickered under their breath but said nothing until after the priest had left. When someone asked me why I had changed the poem and pointed at the priest, I replied that he was sitting in the corner and that was the direction I was supposed to point. No scolding on this one.

By June 1941 I had acquired sufficient English language skills to converse and, if necessary, discuss current events or other with our English speaking young neighbors. Prior to June 18, for several weeks we had all been talking about the upcoming title fight between the champ, Joe Louis and the contender, Billy Conn. The white neighbors, English speaking, were backing Billy Conn while the majority of us, the Spanish speaking folks, were more sympathetic to "the Brown Bomber".

While Tío Esteban was deaf as a result of the previous railroad accident which scarred him for life and deprived him of his hearing, he always listened to the Friday night fights whenever the rest of the men tuned in. This occurred on nights when we were not involved in storytelling activities. He also did not understand English well but was a fight fan nevertheless. Tío Zacarías also was a member of this audience although he too did not speak a great deal of English he did understand more than he spoke.

Following all the discussions about who would win this fight, which lasted for weeks, the big night finally arrived. We were all glued to the new upgraded radio, a console model. We were not literally glued, of course, but all sat around the radio eager to hear the fight. The announcer introduced the fighters and we could hear the cheers for Billy Conn from up the street from the white neighbors even though they lived a block away. There was no similar outburst for the Champ but we all knew he would win and we would cheer his punches. The atmosphere was charged with electricity and cigarette smoke much like it would have been in the actual arena. All present were on the edge of their chairs eagerly awaiting the action as announced from ringside.

In this fight, unlike most of his previous battles, Joe Louis was getting hammered by a fast punching contender. The champ was trailing most of the fight and by the 12th round it was looking like the Champ was in real danger of losing his title. Then, bang, in the 13th round the contender tried to finish off the Champ who somehow found a reserve of energy and courage and promptly knocked out Billy Conn. As the referee counted to ten, cheers started to reach our house. When the final count ended and the radio announcer declared Louis the winner and still champion, we all felt relieved that our champion had again prevailed.

The mood of our white neighbors was dismal at best. Their great white hope had faltered and they felt let down. The prevalent notion was that if the fight had been only 12 rounds," they" would have won. In the world of could have been, they were possibly right but title fights in that era were scheduled for a longer fight. In later years we might have been able to watch these fights on television but at this point in our history, we didn't have access to TV. Color TV was not even a notion that we would have entertained since we were not even tuned in to black and white TV, to watch fights like the one just mentioned.

A REAL BULL STORY

One of Tío Esteban's adventures occurred to him at around age 12.

He said that he was gathering firewood in a pasture where the *ranchero* kept fighting bulls. As he gathered a large amount of branches and large twigs, he noticed that a bull was walking toward him.

He started running toward the fence hoping to outrun the bull. Most bulls run very fast and this one was no exception. As he saw that he could not beat the bull to the fence and not wanting to abandon his stack of firewood, he set the bundle on the ground and hid behind it.

As he lay there quiet and motionless, the bull sniffed at the wood and pushed the bundle around a bit and after a little while, which must have seemed like an eternity to him, trotted off.

Firewood still in his arms, Tío Esteban dashed home shaking like an old model T. Fighting bulls are ferocious and considered fearless and mean. He would have had no chance at survival if the bull had decided to really attack him.

His mother's arms were comforting, but her advice was not. "Stay out of that pasture," she said. "But if you go back for firewood, be sure that one of your sisters is with you."

A CALL FROM NATURE

My grandmother María had a knack for telling stories—especially scary ones.

One night she found the perfect setting to tell us about a hairy beast, so ugly and nasty that it scared children out of their wits.

By the time she finished, we were so scared we went to bed early.

It had started snowing in the early evening and looked like it would continue for at least a week. As usual, we went to the outhouse before going to bed to avoid getting up in the dark and going out in the cold. This particular night it was very cold and the snow was heavy.

I woke up about 3 a.m. and had to go to the toilet. I knew it was cold and snowy but I just could not ignore the call from nature. I was still thinking about the hairy creature in my grandmother's story as I went out.

I opened the door to the outhouse and had just started to sit down when I felt a hairy mass on my behind.

Determined to not give up without a fight, I reached behind me and swatted whatever was there. The cry of the creature scared me even more than the hairy mass.

It was a yowl of our cat as it flew out the door. The poor cat was just trying to find a warmer place to spend the night. Unfortunately for both of us it had chosen the outhouse for refuge on one of the few nights that I had ventured out.

After that night, I took a flashlight with me whenever I had to go out to the outhouse and checked to see if any hairy beasts were sharing the place with me.

FACE THE MÚSICA

Don't remember the date, month or even the year. It was a Saturday. That much I remember because of the routine that many kids in my age group, that is, between about 10 and 16, practiced most Saturdays. The price of a movie at that time was about 10 or 11 cents and affordable to practically everybody. Somewhat strange that I don't remember the price of admission but at that time you could go to a movie, have popcorn, drink a coke and still have a little left over for a candy bar afterwards.

By this era several of the barrio youth understood enough English to enjoy the cowboy movies and the interminable series that ran one episode per week before the main feature. The series were Batman, and other crime fighters who always faced death at the end of each episode then cheated death in the next episode only to be threatened again every week until the final episode. These episodes always had catchy titles such as "Doom of the rising sun", and many others but these titles escape me right now although they were on the tip of my tongue then.

The Saturday afternoon routine was to attend the Cowboy Movie matinee and spend a cool afternoon out of the summer heat. The usual fare was the typical script of cattle rustlers, the runaway horse or buckboard wagon scene and the hero saving the ranch or cattle for the widow. The heroes were the same ones, the names will mean nothing to anyone today but were real heroes then. Cowboys such as Roy Rogers, Gene Autry, Hoppalong Cassidy, and a couple more whose names even I have forgotten. Interesting too was the duo of the Cisco Kid and Pancho, both nicknames for Francisco. But then, even Don Quijote had a sidekick called Sancho Panza, which sounds similar to Pancho, as in Pancho Villa. It might have been interesting to English speaking moviegoers to see the film starring Frank and his sidekick, Frank. Somewhat confusing.

The traditional campfire scene in most of the cowboy movies featured the Sons of The Pioneers singing a couple of songs as the sun sank slowly in the western sky and the campfire blazed brightly and then faded to dying embers as the musicians took their instruments and disappeared into the twilight.

Didn't matter who the cowboy hero was, this same musical group appeared in almost all the westerns. Talking about this particular group is what generated a most interesting story telling session one evening with the old folks. I never knew where they went or how since the scene was out in the middle of a cattle drive.

The evening under discussion started tamely enough when I was talking about the routine music that was always a part of the Cowboy Movie of the day. I had always liked music but not necessarily the type that came with the typical Cowboy Movie. Anyway after my short speech about the music of the movie the old folks started reminiscing about their younger days.

Up to this evening I had no idea that they, my grandmother, my grandaunt and two granduncles, had actually been performers in the Zarzuelas in Mexico when they were younger and years before they came to America. They talked about how Tía Preciliana played the guitar and she and my grandmother sang. Tíos Esteban and Bernabé were members of the troupe. I already knew about the self reliance of my grandmother and grandaunt who learned to shoot a rifle at a young age and shot wild game that the family ate and about other skills that they had to survive. I did not know about this side of their life until that evening.

By this time in their lives they did not remember much of the music that they had performed but did talk about some of their performances before the revolution. The revolution was an event that drove them out of Mexico. This was one of the most informative and entertaining evenings that I remember although by now even my memories have faded.

ADIVINANZAS[12]

What's black and white and red all over?
And your answer is.........
What's round and has a thousand squares?

And your answer is……

Both of these are riddles or *adivinanzas*

Adivinanzas were handed down from one generation to another as the old folks told them, we learned them. They got a great deal of pleasure in tricking us and eventually telling us what the answer was.

Adivinanzas were riddles in the form of poems.

Chistes, jokes were also major topics and we heard the same jokes many times. I finally got the punch line to a couple of these around my 15th birthday.

Other topics of conversation that involved the younger generation had to do with what we had learned in school. We did not have the vast repertoire of stories that the old folks had.

Adivinanzas are still around and virtually everyone knows at least one. These riddles seem to make more sense in Spanish. For example:

¿Qué sera, qué sería que en la mano lo tenía?

And the answer is __?

Adivinanzas are still popular today, particularly with the advent of the computer.

Today any small child can operate a computer and play games that were not thought of until recently.

Today's riddle is "Do children today have as much fun with a computer games as we did with *cuentos* [13] and *adivinanzas*?"

My answer is NO, but others may disagree.

TELEVISION FINALLY CAME TO THE BARRIO

I was already in high school by the time television finally came to the *barrio.*

We all had heard about the marvelous invention in the 1950s. We had seen the boxes with round windows even in some stores in Pratt, Kansas.

The description that most of us agreed on was that this was the beginning of home movies. That's because that is all we could compare television to—movies on the weekend at the local theater.

That there would be special programs and even local news on the new box was something that we could not envision at the time.

We were not too far off. Watching test patterns was an evening activity that got initial laughs that quickly turned to frustration.

There were not many programs available initially but within a couple of years, there were regular programs available during the day and not only at night, as had been the case previously.

In our area, there were mostly cowboy type programs. Western bands and singers, rodeos, colorful characters with names like "Deputy Dusty", "Freddy Fudd the forest ranger" and other similar shows dominated the airwaves.

The old folks got a small TV set and watched the meager programming available. They understood very little English but enjoyed the programs anyway. I do not think they really understood that the people were not speaking to them personally but rather to the general audience. In any event they enjoyed the black and white offerings which rolled, faded, went blank and suffered all the usual problems associated with television in that era.

Color television was not available until the 1960s long after I had left the *barrio*. By this time there were game shows and soap operas on television. Now we have cultural western programs like the PBR circuit. Professional bull riders only have to stay on the bull for eight seconds which must seem like an eternity to them given the punishment they are enduring on the raging beast trying to get them off their back and onto the ground where the bull can gore them. The popularity of this sport has grown to the point where today some of the bulls have fan clubs. Of course, there are other cultural programs available now and there is a wide variety of programming aimed at virtually every taste. This is a far cry from the programs in the early days which I just mentioned previously. Today programs are available in various languages and are increasing in popularity.

DÍAS DE CAZA

Tío Zacarías and Tío Emilio teamed up to teach me about hunting. To this day, I treasure the time I can spend in the great outdoors hunting.

My first recollections of hunting are of Kansas big game--rabbits.

At the time that my uncles took me hunting, it was primarily for rabbits and pheasants. My contribution to the trek was carrying the game that they shot. They needed to have their hands free in order to shoot.

Many times I got tired just carrying the game but as I got older, I was able to take on the role of hunter and shooter.

My uncles were both excellent shots and taught me well.

We always came home with something to eat whether one or two rabbits or several pheasants and occasionally a few quail. During this era, there were a few deer in the state but it wasn't until many years later—around 1970--that deer hunting was allowed in the state.

One particular day when I was about six or seven years old we had gone hunting west of town on a farm that belonged to a friend of my uncle Emilio. Along about 4 p.m. we still had not scared up anything and were discouraged by the lack of game. We continued to walk through shelterbelts and windbreaks around the farm.

Finally our quest paid off. Within a span of 15 minutes my uncles shot four cottontail rabbits and three pheasants. I was carrying all the game and dragging behind as we walked back to the farmhouse. When my uncles saw that I kept getting further behind, they came back to see if I was okay. I was, but since I was so loaded down, I could not keep up.

When my uncles saw the load that I was carrying, they took the game and carried it the rest of the way. In the exuberance of shooting they had failed to notice the growing load that the smallest hunter was carrying.

WATERFOWL IN KANSAS

Ducks were plentiful in Kansas. Geese were somewhat scarce.

I remember shooting ducks on several occasions but shooting geese was rare.

Farmers in our area were cooperative in allowing us to hunt on their property for rabbits or game birds. Hardly any of them wanted to let us hunt their ponds where the ducks and geese hung out. Many of our farmer friends said that they had their ponds leased to hunting clubs who would not allow outsiders to hunt on their lease.

In the many years of hunting in Kansas, I shot multitudes of pheasants, lots of quail, a mountain of cottontail rabbits but only 25 or so ducks, and 1 or 2 geese. These few waterfowl that I shot were along creeks and not on anyone's pond.

We ate everything that we hunted and in the winter fresh meat was welcome for variety and protein. My grandaunt prepared game in exciting and tasty ways. Today's cooks could use her recipes but unfortunately they were never written and have been lost.

She cooked duck with red chile that gave it a unique taste. I do not know of anyone today that prepares duck in this manner. When my friends cook duck, they first soak the duck in vinegar or orange juice then bake it with orange marmalade or other jelly for moisture and flavor. Geese are usually smoked and are very rich and hearty.

One of our rituals at the end of a day's hunt was the cleaning of the shotguns.

Tío Zacarías usually heated a quart of water that he used to wash out the barrel of his shotgun, an old Winchester Model 12. He generally cleaned the other shotgun, Tío Emilio's, also a Winchester Model 12.

The water that he used was hotter than I could tolerate so I did not wash out the barrels but did clean the other parts of the shotguns and oiled them lightly. Both of these shotguns were of 1920s vintage and are still in the family and in good working condition.

Tío Zacarías died one summer day after a quick trip to the hospital so I lost him both as a mentor and as a hunting partner. He did not live long enough to retire from the railroad and actually went from the job to the hospital.

Tío Emilio was a very avid hunter of upland game and waterfowl but he never got an opportunity to hunt deer, elk or antelope. In later life when I visited the old neighborhood, I usually took him deer, elk, or antelope meat.

I had not shot many elk during his retirement years but I did provide him deer and antelope from my yearly hunting expeditions in Colorado. I shared the little bit of elk that I had been lucky enough to get from my usually fruitless elk hunts.

My father did not hunt or fish, but encouraged me to do so. He did not care much for wild game, but would eat pheasant. Thanks to all of them, I enjoy hunting and hope to continue this sport until I can no longer walk in the mountains or see well enough to shoot properly.

A BIG BLACK DOG

One of my grand uncles, Tío Zacarías, was the senior person on the section gang. He worked there many years and in his later years was assigned to work around the depot (that's railroad station to non-railroaders). Part of his duties involved cleaning up the area where the dining cars on the various passenger trains stopped. This area usually had trash and garbage strewn on the ground, and with the many trains running daily, it was a full time job.

It was customary for senior railroaders to receive less exhaustive assignments as they neared retirement age. Both this grand uncle and Tío Esteban were very senior and having paid their dues, they were now getting lighter work assignments.

Tío Esteban worked at the roundhouse and carried out janitorial duties rather than having to do the heavy lifting associated with most of the other assignments on the roundhouse workgroup, called the "Bull Gang", or on the rip track where these laborers repaired railroad cars. The work was hard and today would be considered a "dirty job". All the parts that were removed and replaced on the rip track were heavy and dangerous to handle. Wheels, brake beams, couplers and even knuckles would seriously injure someone if they fell on a body part.

One day when Tío Zacarías came home from work, he mentioned that a nice black dog had been hanging around him at the depot for a couple of days and did not seem to belong to anyone in particular. He was worried that the dog would get run over by a train or the switch engine working in the yard since many of the trains that were switched required movements down by the depot from the many tracks in the classification yard.

He decided that if no one came to claim the dog in the next day or so, we would rescue him and bring him home. No one came for the dog by Friday, so on Saturday morning, he and I went down to the depot, tied a short rope around the dog's neck, and led him home. I now know that he was a Labrador retriever, but at that time, he was just a big black dog.

We named him *Osito* because he had the color of a bear. He was with us for a couple of years until he mysteriously died one summer day. We thought he had been poisoned by an un-neighborly person down the alley. To this day, I am not thoroughly convinced that this person really poisoned our dog, but this person was rumored to have poisoned dogs before so this thought naturally came up. We did not know why he would do such a thing but other folks had lost dogs in the same manner, and all thought that this same person was responsible.

No one ever investigated these incidents nor ever accused the person but still many former dog owners had the same notion upon the mysterious death of their dog. Perhaps many died of old age or other natural causes, but the unspoken accusations and suspicions persisted.

DOG NUMBER 2

I still remember Tío Emilio walking into the house and pretending to hide something under his jacket.

I knew it would be a good surprise and it was.

It was a very hungry puppy. So we fed him milk and a piece of tortilla soaked in the milk. My uncle said that the puppy was a staghound, a dog normally trained to hunt large animals. A farmer who lived near the site of the train wreck where Tío Emilio had been working, had given him the puppy. He said that it was the smallest one in a litter of 12.

Tío Emilio, who worked in the roundhouse, was periodically promoted to carman helper or machinist helper. Both jobs paid more than his regular job.

On this particular occasion he was sent out with a crew to work on a train wreck and move the cars that had derailed back on the tracks. The crew was gone for three days working on the derailment. The trip was lucrative for my uncle as they were getting overtime pay and putting in many hours.

We named the dog Wimpy, which, as it turned out, was not quite accurate. As the weeks went by, the small puppy got progressively larger. When he was about three months old, he was huge. We knew that he would get bigger, not smaller, so we knew that he would have to go to where there was space for him to run and frolic. We didn't have this type of space available.

A farmer friend of the family who had just lost a dog to old age offered to take our dog. According to my uncle, the dog lived with this farmer for many years.

DON LEOBARDO

His real name was Leobardo Jacobo born 18?? Died 12/14/1946.

In the *barrio*, he was also Don Leopardo.

This was a left-handed way for folks to call attention to his hunchback. So to many, he was simply *El Jorobado.*

Although there was little talk among our family about this old-timer, I have a feeling that he may have been a blood relative to a neighborhood family, the family who had a child with the same given name who died fairly young. Like Don Teófilo, Don Leobardo ate with that family on most occasions but lived by himself down the alley in a little one room house.

When he was not at their table, Don Leobardo was boarding down the street where curiosity was not him but the couple who lived there and their reputation for conducting séances.

How he wound up with a hunched back was a mystery until the day he died. Some said it was the result of a railroad accident, which is quite possible since the railroad had its share of mishaps. Others were more kind and explained that he had been a victim of scoliosis although they did not use this word. Whatever caused his condition must have happened many years before I was born.

MY COUSINS

When I was growing up in the 1940s, I often wondered—never aloud—why I didn't have any cousins. All my buddies in the *barrio* always seemed to be talking about their cousins, their *primos,* their supply seemed limitless.

It was not until I was in high schools in the 1950s that I my first cousin was born. By then it was almost impossible to relate to the new cousin in any buddy fashion.

I can thank Doña María for this. She was born 3/22/1889, died 12/17/1967 and had been widowed since 2/10/1936. Her late husband, whom I never met, was born in the 19ᵗʰ century, 6/5/1872 and died, as mentioned above, in1936 when I was only a few months old.

Doña María was a widow and the matriarch of a large family. Although I remember her as a pleasant woman, she was not really able to cope with life by herself. There were four sons and two daughters in the family.

According to my elders, the oldest daughter spent her teenage years assisting her younger siblings adjust to life. She reportedly had become the *de facto* head of the household at an early age. She was not able to attend school beyond a few years of primary grades.

The three oldest brothers served in WWII and returned home with interesting stories about their survival. The youngest was classified 4F, a designation that indicated he had some condition that exempted him from service. He died at an early age after taking a disability retirement from his job due to a heart condition and severe arthritis.

Both daughters ended up marrying my two formerly bachelor uncles, Tío Emilio and Tío Epifanio. Since they were in their 40s when they got married, they got a late start in family life.

Consequently, I have no cousins my age or even close to my age. My oldest cousin, Elisa, is 13 years younger than me.

So, let me tell you a cousin story.

One summer day, Roberto (Beto), the oldest of the male cousins, was playing around with an old reel type lawnmower. When somehow the reel turned over, it cut his thumb almost all the way off.

My uncle Emilio came running out of his house as my cousin was hollering in pain. Immediately they went to the local hospital to deal with the thumb most of which was hanging from the main part of the hand.

Fortunately the doctor was able to reattach the thumb. My cousin was supposed to return to the doctor's office to see if further surgery might be necessary to get the thumb straight. Of course, he never went back and to this day the thumb is crooked but functional.

My cousins' maternal uncles all moved away after they returned from military service. They didn't realize then that their lack of formal education might hamper them from obtaining high paying jobs. In any event, two of them obtained government jobs, although not high level jobs.

Their oldest uncle, Tío (Lolo) short for Dolores, although he was also called Danny, worked at the U. S. Air Force Academy as a custodian. He retired after 30 years service. He spent his last years in retirement sitting on his porch and looking west at the mountains. His view of the mountains was so spectacular that on many occasions people would stop by and offer to buy his house even though it was not for sale.

His two younger brothers got decent jobs in another city. The last I heard about the family was that all the adults had died. I knew about my uncles and their wives but had little knowledge about the other members of the family.

One of my younger cousins died around 1985 of breast cancer. She was survived by her husband, a pilot who worked as a crop duster, and three sons. My cousins from this family live in Kansas in three of the larger cities.

EXTENDED FAMILY AND OTHER CULTURAL RELATIONSHIPS

In the *barrio* as well as among other Latino populations living elsewhere, there were many relationships that are not accounted for in the mainstream culture. Our first cousins are still "primos hermanos" which denotes a closer relationship than the English version. First cousins are the sons and daughters of uncles and aunts. (Note: In Spanish the male form of a noun is used to denote both sexes. The feminine form is used when only females are mentioned.)

It is possible and, in fact, fairly common for young cousins to be considered aunts and uncles of older cousins due to the hierarchy established within our culture. A brother of a child's parents is an uncle to even the children who would be considered second cousins or however many times removed the person would be under the English system.

Aunts, uncles, cousins, relatives of cousins and others related somewhat remotely by marriage are considered part of the extended family and many times, as previously mentioned, live together in the same household.

In addition to "blood" relatives there were other types of relationships in the *barrio* that did not exist, or at least were not prevalent, in the mainstream culture. The term "godfather" has, in the mainstream society acquired a negative connotation and has become associated with organized crime figures, primarily a head of a criminal mob. Godfathers and godmothers were an important part of the extended family. In many cases they were also blood relatives but need not be related in this manner.

The roles of godparents, "padrinos and madrinas" included social and religious responsibilities. Latinos had many opportunities to have padrinos for events that the Roman Catholic Church thought necessary. When a child was baptized, he or she had padrinos, a male and a female usually a married couple but not necessarily since the padrino might be a relative of the child and the madrina could be a family friend or vice versa. In my particular case, my madrina for baptism lived in another city while one of my uncles was my padrino. These two knew each other but were not married to each other. For the "First Communion" and "Confirmation" padrinos were selected. And finally for marriage, there were padrinos needed.

The custom of having padrinos for these festive occasions also generated a relationship based on this role. The parents of the child and the padrinos became "compadres", a relationship not present in the larger society. A set of parents might have three sets of compadres from the three church events of a child and yet another from the eventual marriage of a son or daughter, also a church event but maybe a civil ceremony. English speaking society called these padrinos "witnesses for most ceremonies and "best man or maid of honor" for the witnesses at a wedding ceremony

In our *barrio* padrinos gave gifts to their godson/goddaughter on birthdays, saints' feast days and treated them as part of their extended family if not blood relatives. The godsons typically were extra nice to their padrinos and held them on a high plateau socially. I remember children whose madrina was my grandmother who when they visited her would kiss her hand upon arrival at the house to visit her.

Compadres likewise treated each other kindly and with high esteem, more so than other neighbors or friends. There seemed to be more comadres than compadres in our neighborhood, I guess, because many were widows. I think that some of these comadres were nor really related via the usual events but were treated as comadres more or less in an honorary manner.

Comadres tended to visit each other much more often than compadres as the males were almost always working and visits were afternoon events during the work day. For special events such as a tamalada (see explanation elsewhere) or feast days, compadres got together for a meal and liquid refreshments. Children were sent to visit compadres when one might be ill or just to keep in touch with them. In an era with no telephones personal visits were the norm.

Compadres from the marriage of sons and daughters indicated a closer relationship that "the in-laws", parents of the bride and of the groom who had little or no contact with each other after the wedding and possibly not even after a grandchild was born. In the prevalent culture, ours, compadres got along fairly well unless it happened to be a Romeo and Juliet situation where the two families were blood enemies or just plain feuding over a real or imagined slight in the distant past.

After telephones became available, it was easier to keep in touch with relatives and compadres. Email now has replaced most other forms of communication and allows persons to keep in touch regardless of physical separation.

One last relationship that I mention is that of the other in-laws, brothers-in–law and sisters-in-law. Cuñado and cuñada connote a familial relationship that the English terms do not. It is difficult to explain these relationships given the mother–in–law jokes and other negative terms that make people think that any in-law is an outlaw and not worthy of respect or acceptance. In-laws were pretty much considered extended family members and included in family functions.

Part Two

The Railroad And
World War II

*And our neighborhood
changed dramatically.*

*Y nuestro barrio
combió para siempre.*

THE RAILROAD INFLUENCE

Historians tell us that by 1940 the Empire of Japan already was building its war arsenal. If this was case—and apparently it was-- we never heard of it in Pratt, Kansas.

Similarly, the Japanese probably never heard of Pratt, Kansas, and if they did, it didn't matter then and probably still doesn't.

The Japanese continued to carry out their war plans.

We continued our own day- to-day operations of working on the railroad.

Then on December 7, 1941, thousands of miles away from Pratt, Kansas, bombs from the Japanese air armada devastated Pearl Harbor.

My father and uncles, like many adults in this country, took over our living room and hovered over the radio for news every evening.

In those days, my father and uncles tried to make sense of the attack on Pearl Harbor. What they didn't know, but soon learned, was that the beginning of World War II was about to have an impact on tiny, isolated, wind-swept Pratt, Kansas, our hometown.

And our *barrio* was to change dramatically.

Prior to the attack on Pearl Harbor, word at the local roundhouse was that railroad operations would continue to decrease and that the local jobs would be eliminated or moved to larger cities.

The downfall of the railroad for the local areas, in reality, had been going on for around two decades.

I remember hearing, from the old folks, many stories about our small town *barrio* population and properties that had declined and in some cases disappeared by the time I was born in 1935.

The heyday of this *barrio* was during the 1920s when more families lived there and there were businesses serving the population. According to my grandmother and grand uncles and grandaunts, there was a small store and even a pool hall, which played host to dances on weekends.

In the 1920s and 30s the railroad, a major employer in our area, needed many employees, as their operations were more labor intensive than in later years. Many employees from the barrio worked at the coalscuttle, sand tower, roundhouse, rip track, train service and other railroad operations. There were 30 or more "Carmen" working on railroad car repair and train inspection.

But by 1940, the year when my memories began to solidify, there were no barrio businesses left and only a few families were still living there.

Thank heavens; the Rock Island Railroad was still there.

By the mid-forties, Pratt Army Air Base, home base to B-29 aircraft, (heavy, long range bombers) was built just three miles north of our town, near Iuka, not a suburb of Pratt.

Both the railroad and the air base contributed to changes that occurred as a result of the Big War. In the 1940s, railroads moved hundreds of trains loaded with our troops and their equipment and supplies. Anything that could pull freight or passenger cars was in use regardless of its condition. Broken down locomotives and passenger cars long past their shelf life were still in use but caused many delays and discomfort for the passengers. The number of trains did require maintenance so employees had to work overtime and long hours on a regular basis.

From my house, the Rock Island Railroad roundhouse, *la casa redonda,* rose vividly on the southeastern horizon, just a couple of blocks away. Blackened by the engine smoke, the roundhouse was dark and semi-ugly. Even the lights inside did little to brighten things. The large windows were anything but clean having accumulated a film over many years of smoky work inside.

But it was home away from home for all of our adults.

The roundhouse never slept.

Some 20 to 30 laborers worked each of the three eight-hour shifts on the roundhouse bull gang. These were employees that performed the day to day operations assisting the skilled workers, Machinists, Carmen, and Electricians.

Laborers maintained the locomotives in operating condition. They lubricated the drive wheel journals, the wheel bearings on the drive wheels, and supplied the locomotives with coal or oil, water, sand and other supplies that were used in the cab of the locomotive.

There was a hierarchy of jobs categorized by skills and pay scales. As usual, the lowest paid and lowest of the lot were the laborers. The next rung up the career ladder was that of the helpers whether Machinist or Carman Helpers. Machinists performed skilled labor by operating a lathe on which they cut gears, turned down brass for journals on locomotives and manufactured other parts that did not require the forging of huge parts.

Machinists also repaired air pumps on locomotives, repairing dynamos and maintaining most systems on locomotives. They inspected locomotives on trains and performed minor repairs while the train was at the station and crews were servicing the cars and the locomotive.

Getting a job as machinists was not easy. It usually was the result of the successful completion of an apprenticeship program that involved on the job training, sometimes as Machinist Helper.

Another semi-skilled position was that of hostler. Hostlers were on the fireman's roster and performed similar duties to firemen but did not go on the road on trains.

In the roundhouse and service area, they moved locomotives and performed duties that required a keen knowledge of steam locomotives. They were responsible for keeping locomotives serviced and ready. This often involved moving locomotives from the roundhouse, turning them on the turntable and getting the steam pressure up to operating levels for the locomotive to go on a train.

Hostler helpers assisted the hostlers in turning locomotives and preparing locomotives for the road. Hostler helpers could, conceivably, become firemen and eventually locomotive engineers. Virtually every skilled position had an apprentice or helper position that a person could begin with and work up to the skilled position and thus earn more money.

Machinist helpers could become machinists. Electrician helpers could become electricians. Carmen helpers could work up to the position of Carman and in later years of employment might become inspectors or wrecker operators. All these positions paid more than did the maintenance of the way positions or the unskilled positions in the roundhouse or on the rip track. By the time I started working on the bull gang, this apprenticeship system was no longer available locally although it was available in Chicago, Kansas City and other major railroad division cities. We actually performed many of the duties that helpers and more experienced employees had performed in previous eras.

By the time I was in high school the workforce was very small compared to that of previous years. Changes in the rolling stock, (locomotives, freight cars and passenger trains) and train traffic, which declined after WWII, caused major reductions in the workforce. As railroad employment declined, so did the population in the barrio although death and old age also contributed to the reduction in the population. A few of the older men retired and moved to other cities to live their final days with a son or daughter.

Where there had been 50 to 75 employees working in the roundhouse, the coal tower area and locomotive maintenance and repair, the advent of oil burning locomotives cut the number of employees needed. This modernization from coal burning locomotives to oil burning locomotives occurred in the late 1930s on the Panhandle Division. On other divisions, the railroads continued to operate both coal and oil burning steam locomotives.

After the war, most of the old rolling stock was scrapped. Steam locomotives were lined up in the railroad yards throughout the country in a funeral procession in 1952 and thereafter on their way to the scrap yard.

One other memory of the class system on the railroad was the pay. Engineers, firemen, conductors, brakemen and other highly paid employees received red paychecks while those of us in the lower pay ranks received green checks. There were no Mexicans or Colored folks in the categories of engineer or conductor. Similarly there were no Carmen or inspectors of these minority groups.

Many years later, mid 1960s, while I taught school during the year, I worked at interesting jobs during the summer. I finally hired out as a switchman on the Santa Fe Railroad in the yard in Argentine, Kansas in 1965, a better paying job. Up to 1965 there had not been a person "of color" in this type of job. I seemed ironic that a minority person would work as a switchman with a Masters degree while the white switchmen had a high school diploma required but not necessarily actually earned.

A Dangerous Job

One afternoon as I passed by the tracks in front of the depot on the way home, a group of men was standing around and watching a particular spot on the track. This was the section crew. They were standing around the front of the depot between the mainline and the passing track.

Nearby was a pile of gravel that had not yet been applied between the rails. A gondola car was on the siding with gravel leaking out the bottom trapdoor. I paid a little more attention even though nothing seemed to be happening while I walked by.

None of the men including my father waved to me, which was sort of odd as I knew all of them and their kids most of whom were classmates or, at least, schoolmates. I waved to them and noticed that they seemed dejected but I continued on my way.

When my dad arrived home from work, he seemed downcast and sad. He was melancholy, much like when they had to unload new ties and got creosote on their skin which burned for hours after washing it off.

This was one of the most dangerous tasks that they performed although none of them thought so at the time.

Creosote has been identified as a carcinogen, but was not so designated at that time. He always had to clean up his hands, arms and face with lard and then scrub with soap and water. Despite these cleanup precautions, he sometimes had a red rash on his skin for several days following this work.

When my mom asked about the day's work, he replied that the crew had been unloading gravel on the track in front of the depot. He said that while unloading the gravel, some lumps had gotten stuck in the trapdoor of the hopper car.

When one of the men got into the car to loosen the gravel so that it would flow out, he fell through the trapdoor and the work train, which was moving slowly at the time, ran over him severing his leg just below his abdomen. He died from loss of blood before the ambulance could get him to the hospital.

The event weighed heavily on all of them since they would have to continue doing this type of dangerous work. The engineer and crew of the work train took time off after this accident. Due to financial considerations, the section crew could not afford to take time off.

The company allowed them time off, a half day with pay to attend the funeral. After this event the section crew was sad for a long time according to my dad when he again spoke of the incident months later.

The fatal accident occurred on a section gang that was composed of representatives from several ethnic groups, including Mexicans, Germans, Greeks, Irishmen, Poles and who knows what other ethnic groups. There were around 20 employees regularly and up to 50 whenever there was a special project going on.

Special projects might include replacing ties on a section several miles long. In these instances there was a work train involved which carried workers, equipment and supplies to the job. On these occasions, my dad was promoted to floating gang foreman and had charge of the project and, for a change, received a little bit higher pay.

Whenever there was a major train derailment, the section hands had to rebuild the right of way with new ties and new rails. At that time the work was all done by hand. Today mostly heavy-duty machines do this work.

When I worked at the roundhouse, I witnessed several minor accidents.

The most common accident in the roundhouse area involved high-pressure air hoses that were not properly hooked up. When the air was turned on, the hose swung up and struck someone on the head, almost always the person that had improperly attached it. Sometimes an employee working with this person also suffered a hit as these hoses swung wildly until the air was turned off.

Falls from the top of railroad cars also claimed several victims. Smashed fingers were very common, as were bruises from running into something or something slipping and nudging someone

In all the years that I worked at the roundhouse, all three shifts including the "Graveyard Shift," I never saw a fatal accident. I did get time off on one occasion when my eyes got burned cleaning out a car containing soda ash. It was painful for a few days.

These accidents are examples of the inherent danger in railroad jobs and the fact that even when workers are careful, accidents happen. Two of my close high school friends who were brakemen, lost limbs while switching cars onto a siding. Neither one was killed on the job.

These accidents did not occur through carelessness or faulty equipment, but rather because of the work surroundings. As an example, stirrups and ladders on the side of railroad cars are extremely slippery when wet.

These two high school friends, who lost limbs, fell while climbing the side of a boxcar and were subsequently run over by the wheel which amputated a leg slightly above the ankle. Fortunately they did not bleed to death on the way to the hospital.

THE CANTALOUPE ACCIDENT

Another railroad accident with less gruesome results occurred on a late summer day.

My mom had been grocery shopping and among her purchases were several Rocky Ford cantaloupes. When she arrived home she put them in a tub filled with cold well water so they could be cool for my father and the family in the evening.

When my father arrived home from work he brought three Rocky Ford cantaloupes with him.

"Now, where did you get those cantaloupes," my mom asked.

"A reefer," he replied, referring to a refrigerated freight car.

What had happened was that car full of cantaloupes had derailed in the yard on a hot cargo fruit train headed east. The Roadmaster, the high official in charge of trains and track, told the section crew to take a few since the fruit might spoil before the car could be repaired.

My mom said "I wondered what the commotion was when I went by the switchman's shack and noticed the one car off the track up a little ways toward the roundhouse".

"I could have saved some money if I had known."

WORLD WAR II

Many, if not most of the eligible men in the neighborhood, served in the armed forces during World War II. Those who did not volunteer were drafted and all lived to return home.

Four sons of one of our best neighbors, Don Martín and Doña Victoria, served in WWII. All four returned relatively healthy despite the fact that two were wounded and one was a prisoner of war for a couple of years.

During the war, families had little plaques in the windows of their homes with a star for each person in the military. Their window attracted a lot of attention since it displayed the plaque with four stars.

My father was exempt from the draft by virtue of having three children and a job essential to the war effort. During the war he worked one shift as switchman several times per week after his regular workday on the section gang, many times serving as foreman and supervising the section hands during the day.

These workdays were in excess of 16 hours per day.

Unfortunately, he was not allowed to keep any of these higher paying jobs after the war. At that time, "Mexicans" were not allowed to work in jobs such as switchman, brakeman, or locomotive engineer as the unions allegedly would not allow it.

There were no *barrio* dwellers in any of these unions or in jobs that paid more than the section or the roundhouse. After the war, my father returned to working only his regular job on the section gang.

After WWII several of the veterans moved to the big city where there were more opportunities for gainful employment. By this time, railroad jobs had already diminished due to the replacement of steam locomotives by less labor intensive diesel locomotives. These had replaced the old coal and oil burning steam locomotives which required a large labor force to maintain them in running condition and to actually run them on trains.

The roundhouse workforce was cut severely and the rip track repairs were fewer than in previous years.

During WWII all rolling stock was in constant use carrying soldiers, supplies and vehicles to seaports where they were shipped overseas. The end of the war ended the need for much of the railroad traffic. Truck traffic increased on the highways moving much of the cargo that trains had formerly carried.

Post war needs were diminished and many former railroaders, who had learned other skills while surviving the war, were now, ready for different jobs. Wichita was the closest urban area that had manufacturing plants needing employees. Many of the returned veterans moved there for new careers with a better future.

During WWII the airbase had brought in many airmen but there was no housing available in town for Hispanic airmen and their families. Those folks in the *barrio* who had space could convert it to a small apartment or room. They managed to provide housing for several families with airmen stationed at the B-29 base north of town.

The old folks in our extended family rented out the little house with two rooms, Tío Esteban's house. A family from San Antonio, Texas rented the house. Winters in the South Texas city were very mild compared to the high wind and snowy days of Kansas, so we often heard them ask: "How do you people survive here in the winter?"

We had no choice, so we did not answer what was mostly a rhetorical question. They stayed for two years. Ricardo, the airman, played trumpet in the band at the base and did not have to go overseas or into combat. His wife was an artist who fashioned department store manikins and painted. She painted, actually used colored chalk, portraits of my mom, and my two uncles. I have no idea where these portraits are today. She also decorated the cupboard doors in the kitchen in the old house.

Our *barrio* did not produce any women veterans. Likewise, there were no women occupying the jobs vacated by the men who volunteered or were drafted. The war changed many things, including the makeup of the barrio.

As veterans left and took their families to the big city, the population figures for the neighborhood dropped. Those who stayed did so because of their seniority, which promised them a job when, they returned from the war.

The available labor force was better educated than before the war. Industry profited from the skills that veterans had gained in the service as well as the education they acquired. Their newly acquired skills contributed to their old employer or in many cases to their new employer. In the modern technological society they would not be highly sought after but at the time, they were better prepared for the types of jobs available than the majority of college graduates of that era.

During the war any available person might be hired for difficult jobs and it was during this time that women obtained better paying jobs. After the war, many women lost their jobs to the returning veterans.

A few women and several persons of Mexican descent managed to keep the jobs that they had acquired during the war and the accompanying labor shortage. No women worked for the railroad in my hometown but there were women hired in other cities.

Two female cousins worked in the Amarillo, Texas roundhouse during the war. They told us that there had been 28 women working in the roundhouse during the war but that they had all lost their jobs after the war.

They were not replaced by 28 men though as the railroad was cutting back and replacing the old steam locomotives with diesels which did not require the same level of maintenance or a roundhouse. Many jobs were eliminated as a result but returning veterans were placed elsewhere as the railroad was obliged to provide them a comparable job when they returned.

Returning veterans mentioned that they had experienced discrimination in military service during the war, WWII. They had experienced this in their hometowns prior to the war and even after although not to the same degree. While in the military they had been exposed to other countries and cultures during service outside the US. Upon their return home, they asserted their newly discovered civil rights- - rights that they had just fought to protect for other Americans.

Gradually they were able to change a few things in town such as the ability to get a store bought haircut, but not many more. We (Mexicans regardless of age)were still not allowed to use the facilities in city parks until years later.

Through organizations such as the Veterans of Foreign Wars (VFW) and the American Legion, changes began to occur. Finally many barrio residents were able to eat in a couple of restaurants downtown due to these efforts. Others did not take advantage of these newfound opportunities due to financial considerations but beer parlors did appear to reap a harvest of new money.

COLLEGE WAS OUT OF THE QUESTION

The end of World War II produced the GI Bill, which opened the doors to colleges and universities for many Hispanics.

That was not the case in our *barrio*.

Few individuals in our neighborhood had notions of obtaining a college education since it was expensive, required a high school education and was not seen as a necessity for the type of jobs available to them.

No one in the barrio had expressed an interest in becoming a doctor or lawyer, both requiring college degrees and post-graduate work involving a few extra years in school.

A college degree seemed like an unrealistic goal for most people in the *barrio*. Besides a high school diploma, entry to college required financial aid as well as a strong desire. Most *barrio* residents did not have a high school diploma and thus did not meet the threshold eligibility.

Those of us who went to college did so with scholarship assistance.

Teachers, who now have college degrees, at that time, could teach with a 60-hour certificate.

There were still one-room schoolhouses in operation in the county and throughout the state.

Registered Nurses (RNs) had college degrees but one could enter the profession with a Licensed Practical Nurse (LPN) certificate. LPNs were supervised by an RN.

This is how my mother started her first career outside the home.

PART THREE

UNFORGETTABLE NEIGHBORS

*Even after 60 years, I still have
a vivid picture of my neighbors.*

◆

*Después de 60 años todavía me acuerdo
de mis vecinos como si fuera ayer.*

Among the many things that I remember from my early years are the quaint characters that lived in the *barrio*.

They must have made an everlasting impression on me because even after more than 60 years, I still picture them in my mind and can see them as vividly as when they were alive. I will describe several of them in hopes that someone else will derive some pleasure at meeting these characters.

They all died years ago so they will not be correcting my impressions of them.

OUR FAVORITE NEIGHBORS

Our favorite neighbors lived right next door.

Don Martín and Doña Victoria were the patriarchs of the barrio. They were the oldest couple, and in my eye, wisest.

They had unofficially adopted my father when he came to the barrio as a young immigrant with no family there or even any acquaintances in town. I heard that they introduced him to my mother but I was never able to verify it.

They had five sons of their own and one more mouth to feed seemed to be a natural extension of their family and generosity. Always pleasant, they served as barrio grandparents to any and all--except for those who were rude to their elders.

Since they lived next door, we often shared advice and vegetables. Don Martín often talked about La Trementina, a small town in New Mexico where they had lived before coming to Kansas.

When I think of Don Martín, the first thing I see is his moustache. He always kept it trimmed short and never allowed it to grow long or droop. This was in contrast to his balding head where there were a half dozen white hairs randomly arranged.

Doña Victoria, on the other hand, had long hair and wore it in a braid, a bun, or two braids rounded up and tied in the back. Most of the adult women in the *barrio* wore their hair long.

They certainly were a couple who deserved to be called "Don" and "Doña". They always dressed up anytime they went to town and to church even when the church was the little mission a few doors away.

Most of the time, we wore clothes that now would be in vogue because of their threadbare appearance.

Moreover, Don Martín and Doña Victoria were the only couple I know who had *tataranietos.* If the word is a tongue twister, it is because it means that they had great-great-great grandchildren. Don Martin and Doña Victoria lived to celebrate their 75th wedding anniversary, a truly great feat for anyone.

Unfortunately, I left the barrio shortly thereafter. I have not been able to locate them while visiting family graves in the local cemetery. The dates of their birth and death are not available and they may be buried elsewhere.

Today not even their old house remains to signal their existence. These patriarchs of the barrio were never replaced but rather left a void in the social structure of the community that no one else filled. Respect for our elders has always been a family and community value and this couple earned it and valued it.

NICKNAMES AND SOBRENOMBRES[14]

It seemed like everyone in our *barrio* had a nickname, what we call *sobrenombre,* in Spanish. How some people got their nickname was easy, most of the time, for it usually was associated with some feature.

For example, *el gordo* was a tag for someone with extra weight.

Sometimes, it was not so easy to guess the origin of someone's nickname. Take for example, Junior, a relative of Don Martín and Doña Victoria. He was known as *El Tuna.* This may have been because somewhere along the way, someone could not say junior and it came out "junia" or tuna.

It may have been because he was a chubby kid. Whatever the reason, he carried the nickname in the barrio and eventually no one remembered his real name. Since he lived in another city we did not have daily contact with him so did not learn his real name.

Nicknames are not always based on anything in particular. This tuna lived in the big city and worked for a dairy. On occasions he visited the barrio. Both he and his sister, a very pretty young woman, were older than most of us and seldom visited in the barrio. I only mention him because he was the first Tuna that I knew of. The other one was an NFL coach.

EL GALLITO

Despite the seemingly masculine nickname, which translates to The Little Rooster, this person was a girl.

Her grandparents, Don Martín and Doña Victoria, were as I said before, two of the nicest people ever. Her parents were nice, not exceptionally so, but at least they were not hostile. She was hostile in spite of or because she was not particularly attractive.

How this girl received her nickname is still a mystery. Her right eye had a mind of its own and sort of faced to the side much like a chicken's eye. In later life she wore glasses that improved her eyesight but it didn't straighten out her *ojo tuerto.*

Perhaps this was a motive for the nickname.

She was also very feisty much like a fighting rooster so this may have influenced the nickname. On some days her disposition was nasty but on other days it was tolerable.

She was not friendly to anyone and even talked back to her parents and grandparents.

This in itself was sinful in this era as we were commanded by the church and the older folks to honor and obey but not to sass our elders. It was okay to disagree with peers but not with adults whether relatives or just acquaintances of the family.

This girl never went beyond grade school while she lived in the barrio, but since her parents moved to another town nearby, she might have continued her education elsewhere.

There were not many social events in the barrio for young persons but one that I remember involving her was a Halloween wiener roast to be followed by a midnight show at one of the local theaters.

My brother, my sister, and I were invited to her party. Our parents gave us permission to attend one of the two events but not both. We opted for the wiener roast in hopes that our folks would later change their mind and let us attend the midnight movie. The hot dogs were good and the other stuff was also edible. We returned home early and stayed up late waiting for the permission to go to the midnight show. It never arrived so we went to bed disappointed.

CLARITA: LA NO MUY BONITA

Clarita was somewhat of a foster child. She lived with an older couple, not her birth parents. This older couple looked after her for many years.

She and her foster father bore an uncanny resemblance to each other. Her birth mother was unknown except, of course, to her foster parents.

Although her exact origins were largely unknown, speculations ran rampant regarding her lineage. There were many rumors floating around as to who were her real mother and her real father. Her manners and her financial status can only be described as poor.

She was a very light skinned person, similar in color to the family of her foster father's brother. In fact, she was one of the lightest skinned persons in the barrio. Like her first cousin, *El Gallito, she* was not friendly and not steeped in social graces.

She was a member of a very extended family that I venture to say covered about forty percent of the *barrio* residents. By virtue of unofficial adoption, but more than likely by birth, she was a member of the New Mexico clan headed by Don Martín and Doña Victoria.

Even if she had inherited niceness, she would have needed more than her share to overcome deficits and make a difference socially. Even when her cousin gave a party, she was not invited.

I never saw her at the *barrio* church "mission," which was literally in her backyard. And she never attended school either.

OUR OWN "FATS"

Everyone knows someone called Fats, whether Minnesota Fats, Domino or whatever "Fats."

El gordo, a particularly chunky guy in the *barrio,* wore the largest denim overalls (*lonas*[15]) I had ever seen up to that time. At least two of the fatter kids, one other plus me, could have fit in his pant legs and still have had room left at the bib.

When he walked, he seemed to sort of ripple and could almost literally meet himself coming and going. *El Gordo* was definitely a good-natured guy, always smiled and acted like he would enjoy the day despite what ills might befall him.

As I now think about it, his smile may have been due more to heartburn than to joviality. This interpretation of smiles is accurate for many small infants.

El Gordo had few musical talents that but he always seemed to fit in at social gatherings, along with the more musically talented, like Lee the Flea, formerly a member of the Mad Hawaiians a small group featuring two guitars and sometimes, a mandolin or violin.

I never found out what he did for a living although he went to work every day. In later years, the WWII era, he left the barrio to move to the big city of Wichita. I did not see him again until his mother's funeral. This was a few years later and he had slimmed down a bit by then. Somehow, he did not loom as large as he had when we were smaller kids.

In the *barrio,* all of us noted that he and his brothers had the same last name with the exception of the youngest member of the family. Perhaps this young man, Bobby A was a stepson.

In any event this young man was one of the first, and for a long time, maybe the only *barrio* dweller to go to college. There was a rumor floating around that he played basketball at Wichita University. No one ever confirmed the rumor nor actually saw him play. He was not the tallest kid around so we doubted that he could play college basketball. In addition, he had not played even in high school and we were not aware that he had attended high school, at least not in Pratt.

AND THEN THERE WAS VIC

Vic was one of *El Gordo's* younger brothers, of which there were around four. (See previous note about Bobby A, the possible youngest brother)

Vic worked for the city sanitation department and along with a few others in the barrio, came home for lunch in a city truck. Two of his relatives also worked for the city and at noon the front yard looked like the city trash truck parking lot and staging area for a fly invasion of the *barrio.*

And one other thing, all of Vic's family had light skin. They definitely did not look like those of us who were darker. Their mother was a fair skinned blonde with a nice disposition who did not venture out of the house very often. Given the harsh Kansas sun, this probably kept her from getting sunburned. No one would have mistaken them for Scandinavians but compared to most of us, they were very light and could have passed for some race other than what we all were.

Vic cultivated *chiles*, tomatoes, cucumbers, squash, onions, garlic, cantaloupes and watermelons. The rest of the barrio gardeners specialized and grew only two or three vegetables. Despite the largesse from the garden, no other barrio resident received gifts of vegetables from him as they did from others who were either more generous or simply had surpluses they wished to get rid of.

Neither of his two sons liked to work in the garden or even to eat what the garden produced. In this trait they were very much like the rest of the young guys in the *barrio.* Stoop labor was not our hobby or avocation. While we were obliged to work in the garden, it was more out of necessity than actual interest.

The only good garden work that I can remember was watering the *chile* and harvesting in the days following the onset of fall. Many of the neighborhood gardeners pulled the *chile* plants out of the ground and stacked them in large piles in the *huerta* [16] to pluck a few leftover *chiles* after the first frost of the year. All the ripe *chiles* had already been harvested prior to this last operation of stacking the plants. By this time of year all other garden products were canned, dried or otherwise preserved.

Although Vic started working in the sanitation department, he eventually was reassigned to the water department and learned plumbing without going through a formal apprenticeship.

He was the first Mexican to work anywhere in the city services other than the sanitation department. Vic was one of many WWII veterans in the barrio, all of whom served with distinction. Later on there were others who found jobs with the city and learned a trade such as plumbing but none finished the informal apprenticeship program to become master anything and so did not earn the higher salaries. The trades they were able to learn were not through regular apprenticeship programs as none existed but they did get on-the-job training that enabled them to perform the varied duties.

Vic died years ago at a fairly young age and there is no trace of the family or their properties anywhere in the *barrio* today. His gravestone states that he was born 3/31/1921 and died 10/24/96. His brother, who was killed in the Vietnam War, was the youngest of his family to die. Others lived well into their 80s. Vic's wife "Tillie" real name unknown was born 11/28/1923 and died 11/23/1986. Both are buried side by side in the local cemetery.

Vic's uncle, Don Abrán, (Mr. Abraham) hosted poker games on some Sundays and other occasions in the root cellar located in his yard within walking distance of the outhouse and the kitchen. Mr. Abe, as the neighbors called him, always took a house cut of every pot, which amounted to around 10 percent.

He was the only who made any money on the games. All other participants lost money although the amounts weren't large. Vic's garden was a showpiece in the barrio and Mr. Abe picked choice vegetables daily but never worked in the garden. He claimed he had a tic in his neck and face.

"I have St. Vitus Dance," he would say and none of us knew how to dispute his medical diagnosis. Born José Abrán Montaño 7/21/1883 he died 12/3/1977.

ONE MORE BROTHER

El Caraveo[17], another brother of *El Gordo,* was tall and light complexioned.

Although he didn't come out and say it, *El Caraveo* saw himself as a handsome devil of a guy.

What he would boast of was that he was a great musician.

Well, let's say that he played the guitar--not well, but seemingly pleasing to the listeners, most of whom had not yet heard Chet Atkins [18]or Andrés Segovia.[19]

At that time anyone whose guitar had all six strings was considered musically astute. He had soirées in his yard and provided "music" but all those who attended brought their own beer. Minors, of course, brought soft drinks but occasionally sneaked a beer. He also discoursed on a multitude of topics and was the authority on anything he felt knowledgeable about.

Unlike his brothers, he did not garden, did not work for the city and had no visible means of support but always had money. Perhaps he gambled and always won, likely not in Mr. Abe's cellar.

He often attempted to instruct us younger guys on how to properly play the guitar. "G7", he often instructed, "play a G7 chord".

Other times he concentrated on a G diminished chord. Our interest also diminished. We were never sure he actually knew the difference but did know the names. Actually most of his playing would more properly be considered discord.

As a musician, he was a distant fifth in the barrio, not to be confused with the size of container, which frequently appeared at his side. We noted that he never played at any of the many dances held in the garage down the alley. He did not appear to read music and played strictly by ear.

No one was sure he could read Spanish or English since we never saw him with any reading material.

He surely would have been appalled and highly incensed if he ever heard us call him *Carafeo* (ugly face) rather than his actual name, which no one knew anyway. *El Caraveo* was the only name that we knew for him.

THE FLEA COULD PLAY

Lee, "the Flea", one of the younger sons of Don Martín and Doña Victoria, was a musician extraordinaire.

Lee played the mandolin, the guitar and most anything else with strings. He played for dances and entertained often. Lee played many different styles, from country western to church music.

He could read music but not enough to overshadow his good ear and natural talent. He could play virtually anything; if he heard it, he could play it and well at that. Lee played with several groups in various types of establishments, such as bars and neighborhood dances.

During his performances, he kept his liquid intake constant and drank whatever beer was available or munched a taco to keep his strength up. His taste in beer was not exclusive and he seemed to favor free beer. Much of the time he played for his own amusement sitting on his porch and sipping a few beers in the evening.

Lee also had the first bathing shower in the *barrio* shortly before the city extended the water line to our area. As natural gas became available, coal and oil stoves were replaced, but he utilized solar heat for the shower since it was outside.

The shower stall was a narrow, tall box with a curtain for a door and a 55 gallon drum for water storage and heating. There was no temperature control other than waiting for the proper time in the afternoon or evening and hoping that the ambient temperature had not gotten the water to a merely scalding temperature.

It required a good judgment to add enough cold water from a hose to temper the water that had absorbed solar heat all day in August. Usually the water was too hot or quite cool and made for a quick shower. Later on he installed a regular bathroom in his house but due to constant migrations to California and back, he probably did not use it a lot.

A kleptomaniac with a fetish for clothes could have made off with a varied wardrobe by just waiting for someone to take a shower and grabbing the clothes which hung outside the shower stall.

Lee never got stressed out and probably would have walked back into the house naked, or perhaps to someone's house to report the theft if a thief did steal his clothes. He would not have reacted violently nor even gotten angry, he simply would have had a cold beer and played his guitar, maybe before getting dressed again.

Other barrio residents also rigged up showers at about that time, copying to some extent Lee's shower stall model.

Our household too enjoyed the summer showers both natural and artificial. In cold weather the outdoor showers got to be more infrequent due to the ambient temperature and the water temperature. Showering was okay but drying was uncomfortable.

A cold north wind would discourage all but the frozen few from taking showers outside. In later years even after indoor plumbing came to the *barrio*, outhouses continued in use for several years

Lee's wife, Broda, née Aurora, born 4/21/1919 died 11/9/97 was an overbearing woman who truly did not appreciate his talents or his gentle manner. She did not like to stay in one place very long, so she nagged Lee to go to greener pastures.

They moved in and out of state several times, usually selling everything they owned prior to leaving town. When they returned naturally they had to buy all new furnishings. Neither had a profession but seemed to get jobs they wanted despite their lack of skill in any particular field.

Lee worked at various jobs from hospital orderly to railroad "gandy dancer," a semi-derogatory term applied to section workers on the railroad. The term is hardly used today as section workers now are skilled machine operators, albeit still the lower paid workers on railroads.

Because of his physical condition, Lee never lasted too long at any job, even union jobs. Despite this, Lee and his wife always seemed to have enough money to live well.

Broda worked a little, smoked a lot and traded Comic books with the other patrons of literature.

Word in the *barrio*—and, of course, there were always rumors--was that she had a daughter from a youthful fling and had given her up to be raised by an elderly couple down the street.

If this sounds somewhat familiar, it is because this is where Clarita comes into the picture.

Well, if nothing else, the connection seemed like a fit—as far as the *barrio* wags were concerned.

And people in the *barrio* liked the story so well that it stuck as if it were the gospel truth.

A summer weekend evening involving Lee and music might include a dance in Pete's garage on a Saturday night. The concrete floor wore down the soles of dancers' shoes but they danced the night away despite this.

Lee, and at least one other musician, mostly my father, played an interesting selection of waltzes, polkas and *corridos.*

There were no ballroom quality dancers in the barrio; nevertheless, participants enjoyed themselves and thought that they were good dancers.

Pete's garage was the only paved garage, with coarse cement for a floor. All other garages in the barrio had dirt floors. There were only four or so garages besides his so it was in demand.

There were few recreational opportunities available to the folks so, in essence, they created their own. The younger set learned a couple of dance steps by watching their elders and imitating them as best they could.

The *tacuachito,* a step or method of dancing popular in rural New Mexico, also became popular in the barrio. It consisted of mainly positioning the couple side by side rather than face to face and was adaptable to most music although it would not have been adequate for a Viennese Waltz. It may have been the precursor of Rock and Roll and later styles of music where dancing is more an individual movement and does not really need a partner, as there is more physical contact with groups rather than with partners.

A few beers for the musicians, actually Lee since my father didn't drink, usually encouraged them to play a little bit longer. Lee was obliged to consume the beer by himself. He didn't want to offend the persons who had provided it. If there had actually been a charge for playing, it would not have been exorbitant but they never charged since no one actually sponsored the event.

And whom would they have charged anyway?

My father who almost always accompanied Lee at the dances was a self taught guitarist of notable talent.

It was surprising that men who had worked hard all week on heavy physical labor had so much energy left for the weekend to spend much of it dancing on Friday or Saturday nights. The women all worked in the home and had energy left over for weekends. According to my last survey of the cemetery Bernard "Lee" Blea was born 6/8/1919 and is not listed as buried indicating that he may be alive and living elsewhere, or perhaps, buried somewhere in New Mexico.

RACCOON CAPTOR

One particular incident involving Lee that sticks in my mind is the "Raccoon Caper."

Lee had gone hunting with my uncles and me on several occasions and he always remarked about our marksmanship. Both uncles who took me hunting were excellent marksmen but they worked during the day.

Lee complimented me several times on my accurate shooting and particularly that I usually shot pheasants in the head and did not tear up the body. It was not always by design but I almost always tried to lead the flying bird a little more than the other hunters for that very reason. I was mostly successful so he was impressed.

One fall day he came to the house and asked me to bring a 22 caliber rifle and follow him. I did so and we ended up at his garage. I wondered why he wanted my rifle since he had a 12 gauge shotgun of his own, and this would be adequate for any type of shooting he might need to do.

When we arrived at his garage, he pointed to a loft, a kind of ledge, in the garage and showed me a huge ugly raccoon that was lying there.

He explained that this raccoon had been attacking his dogs, tearing up the trashcans and destroying other things in his yard and garden and gaining weight. He was afraid the animal might have rabies and wanted him out of there.

I complied with his request and we removed it from his garage. The beast was a very large raccoon that was obviously well fed. His dogs were quiet after that.

There were no further raccoon invasions that year, or in succeeding years that I can recall.

El Mocho

El Mocho acquired his nickname due to an accident involving an old-fashioned wringer washing machine.

This particular machine was an early model that had a gearshift lever on the side to change the speed of the agitator. It also had a wringer above the tub where the operator wrung out the clothes prior to hanging them out to dry on a clothesline. This model washing machine may not even exist anymore unless one could find a similar one in an antique store or junkyard. Modern washers bear no resemblance to these early models.

El Mocho was a young kid when one day as he was toddling around the washing machine, he stuck his right thumb near the belt that was driving the agitator. His right thumb got caught between the pulley and the belt and these snipped off his thumb.

His brother, *el Sapo*, was called that because of his pudgy shape much like a toad.

All of the foregoing are actual nicknames of persons that I knew when they lived in this particular barrio.

Some of the residents had more than one nickname and different persons called him or her by the nickname known only to them or used only by them. For example, there was Colchas, a nickname for Asención whose main nickname was "Satch", or *Chon*, depending on who he was talking to at that moment.

From A to Z: Still Weird

Although Xenón begins with an X, it is pronounced Zenón. Xenón is not an inert gas although this Xenón was pretty much inert most of the time.

To my knowledge, he never worked at anything while he lived in the *barrio*. Neither Xenón nor his two brothers, Raimundo and Benino worked at a job but rather spent their days hanging around apparently watching/helping each other rest.

Benino was a nasty type who scolded young children and pretended to know a lot. We usually referred to him as *"veneno"* rather than Benino since we considered him poison.

Benino was a physically striking person. This does not mean that he hit us or anything like that. He had a notable physical characteristic that set him apart and made him different. His head leaned to one side and he looked like he was taking a nap as he sat, stood or even while he walked. Occasionally he tossed his head to the left and it did move but always came back to rest on his right shoulder.

Maybe his nasty disposition was due to his physical condition.

Another feature that stood out was his very high forehead. His hairline started about level with his ears, and if you drew an imaginary line between them over the top of his scalp. *Veneno*—Oops, I mean Benino-- was not the most popular older guy in the *barrio*.

Suffice it to say, that when the family finally moved on, everyone was glad to see all of them go. Perhaps *el Caraveo* was sad to see him go as he was one of a few who hung out with him. Both of these guys were pompous and overbearing besides being smug and untalented.

Raimundo was outstanding in his use of language not usually found in a dictionary. He did not speak grammatically correct nor coherent Spanish. Even though he wore a cap which would have been more at home on an impoverished professor's skull, when he opened his mouth, anyone could tell that he was not a professor or even literate.

He used words that he must have invented for the occasion because he did not know the correct word.

One of his oddest utterances dealt with the Japanese. While the word *Japoneses* is the correct Spanish word for them, he referred to them as the *"Chapanises"* which had a splash from both English and Spanish.

He had many stories to tell and told them constantly to anyone who passed by or came near him. He often talked about his missionary work in west Texas.

The brothers had a sister named Cruz who appeared to be the family's cross-to- bear. Their matriarch claimed to be related to a nice neighborhood woman who had problems of her own before the appearance of the relatives.

Cruz was a mousy, plain, quiet, *gordita*. She resembled her mother in most aspects except, perhaps, weight. Both were about four-foot-nine and dumpy.

Lacking any identifying marks like tattoos or a hooked nose, she made up for it by talking so softly that no one could hear her from more than a few feet away unlike her brothers who talked quite loudly. Perhaps, like her brothers, she really had nothing to say.

She too appeared to do nothing and may have served an idleness apprenticeship with her brothers. If there was a father, I never heard of one, although there must have been one somewhere along the way.

Some of the younger kids with wilder imaginations thought that maybe the family had fled to Kansas after disposing of their father. Most of us thought that this was too far- fetched, as they claimed they had no money, insurance or other.

Momma bear, the matriarch of the clan, was a short chunky woman with no visible scars or moles. She claimed to be an excellent cook and often stated that she had previously cooked for ranch hands.

"They just loved my cooking," she would boast.

The family was semi-migrant. That is, they moved around a lot but only after they had exhausted their welcome at other people's homes. The process was in action in this instance. In addition to pretending that the matriarch was a "blood relative" of our neighbor, the family proclaimed to all within earshot that they were bearers of the gospel and that the Lord had sent them.

No member of the family ever conducted services nor performed any action that one might expect of a person of the cloth.

They said that they were from somewhere in west Texas, possibly the town of Muleshoe but they never specified which dusty town they had actually lived in. None of them admitted to a high school education and if they had, few would have believed them.

Neither Xenón nor Raimundo ever lifted a finger to help their "aunt"; their mother's long lost cousin. They seemed to not notice that there were chores to perform in the household where they were staying. One of the family residents, el Sapo, complained that his "cousins" had increased his chores and that they did nothing other than eat, sleep and complain about the weather.

The family departed on a crisp fall day stating that the Lord wanted them to spread the gospel in a warmer climate. This was fortunate for all concerned because the crowded house had become increasingly hostile with the visitors only adding to the expenses and workload. We never saw them again, not that anyone particularly looked for them to return. The lady of the household seemed pleased that her alleged long lost cousin was again lost.

WHITE FAMILY IN THE BARRIO

Up until I started school when I was five, I assumed that everyone spoke Spanish.

Oh, I knew that other people spoke English, a language I assumed was reserved for adults like my parents and uncles who sometimes listened to the radio in English, especially during World War II.

All of that changed when a white family with two or three kids moved into the *barrio*. They were recent arrivals and did not stay very long, at least not long enough for me to find out how many there actually were in the family.

They did not speak Spanish. I did not speak English. But hand signals and gestures worked well for playing together.

There were two other non-Hispanic, English-speaking families in the *barrio*.

These were two black families. Both families learned enough Spanish to get by, although I recall that members of one family had problems pronouncing some words. A quick example was their pronunciation of "*pueblo*" which they pronounced "*pópulo*."

The other family moved their trailer home after about a year and left for California. They had learned enough Spanish to barely carry on limited conversations.

But it didn't take long for one of the black mothers to gain a Spanish nickname. The *barrio* wags called her *La Leona*, her name was actually *Leona*.

She was fierce, much like a lioness, so we felt the nickname was appropriate. Larger than even her husband, she was, we felt, too severe with her children. We often watched and cringed as she cut a small branch from a handy tree to assist the children in hurrying home.

This type of parental control, unfortunately, took its toll on one of her sons, who wound up spending a couple of years in the state reformatory for boys.

While we never saw her take a switch to her husband in public, we heard enough loud commotion some Friday nights after he came home with a few too many drinks.

While I was away, in Navy Flight Training, the teenaged girl in this family left quite a dent in my memory—and on my car. As related by my sister who was present, this girl lost control of a car she was driving one evening, while learning to drive, and plowed into my auto, which was parked in front of our "new" house.

She left the scene of the accident but later returned with her father, who came armed with a sixteen-pound sledgehammer to "repair" my car. My sister, who was driving my car while I was in the Navy, wisely stopped the repair effort in time. By the time I got back from the service, the car had been scrapped.

I also recall an older Negro, which is one of the terms that was used for African Americans at that time; the other term of those times was "colored."

He was quite popular with the youths of the *barrio* because he played checkers with us all the time. He won most of the time, which is what an adult is supposed to do, so it didn't matter much at the time.

What was interesting of this racial mix is that despite our limited English and their broken Spanish, there was enough overlap to understand most things. Later with the advent of television, the English fluency of the Spanish speakers improved considerably.

The Catholic School library consisted of a few books but none of any particular interest so it did not help me much in learning English during the first years that I attended classes there.

A ROCK BY ANY NAME

Petra, Pietro, Pedro, *piedra*, Pierre et al. (1935-2004)

All of these names refer to a rock starting with St. Peter or a rock in the far distant past.

My friend Pierre (Pete) was an adventurer from a very early age. He was the only kid in the eighth grade that drove.

He had an old Plymouth pickup that was, at best, junk. It served his purpose, which was largely hauling hay for the horses that his father owned. His next younger brother was the one who should have been named after a rock. I'll tell you more about him later.

This particular event is neither about the truck nor about the day that it stalled on the railroad tracks, but rather about a different vehicle.

One summer day when I was around 13 years old, a cloud of dust swept down the street in front of the old house. A motorcycle settled in amidst the dust and there was my classmate from Sacred Heart School (SHS) Pierre. He had "borrowed" a motorcycle from someone who worked for his dad, who owned a gasoline station and other businesses.

"Hop on and I'll take you for a ride," he said.

I remember wondering whether he had any knowledge of driving a motorcycle but I figured that anyone who worked with horses, and drove a truck while hauling hay in the country was probably, okay as a motorcycle maniac.

With no thoughts about helmets since there weren't any at the time and no thoughts about personal safety, I climbed on the back and off we went.

I had expected a short ride around the barrio where there was very little traffic and dirt streets precluded high speed. The first thing Pierre did was to head for the highway, US281, a connector to the Pan American Highway.

I still expected a short pleasant ride.

My surprise grew as our speed increased. I couldn't hear anything Pierre tried to tell me since I was hanging onto him and the back of the seat.

I do remember something about, "this machine will easily do 100 mph," but the words flew by as we gained speed.

I knew that we would not go very far at any speed as we headed north because there was a major bend in the road as it went around the old airbase. After a mile or two as we approached the airbase, Pierre slowed to a speed at which we could again talk a bit.

"Sorry," he said disappointed. "I could only get it to do 95 miles per hour."

I was relieved. But not for long.

On the way back to town, he tried to break the century mark once more.

"This lousy bike couldn't run worth a dime," he said when we got to my house. He stopped and I got off.

"I better get this bike back before the owner finds out it is gone," Pierre said as he drove off, confirming my suspicions of his "borrowing" ways.

THIRTY BALES OF HAY

In the *barrio,* we referred to Pierre, my good buddy, as that "wild and crazy guy."

And if you can believe it, his next younger brother, Elmo, was even crazier and wilder. Elmo played baseball although not well. He was a catcher who couldn't catch and always blamed the pitcher when he dropped the ball which was most of the time. His excuse was that the pitcher did not throw the ball fast enough to stick in his glove. He later became a bull rider many years before it became a money making sport and bull riders were revered by adoring fans. Even the bulls today have fan clubs.

On this occasion Pete and I had gone to a hayfield south of town and loaded up around 30 bales of hay on the truck. I looked at the old truck and then the hay. It was piled several bales high. The hay seemed about 100 bales high, even though we had stacked it and interlocked it so that the weight of the top ones kept the bottom ones packed somewhat tightly. "Hey, Frank, that was my nickname at the time, why don't you get on top of the hay? I want to make sure it doesn't fall off."

Pete kept asking me to get on top of the hay. I decided that I did not want to do this because it looked to me that the hay would shift and I would go tumbling down with the hay, possibly under it. We proceeded toward the barn a couple of miles distant absent anyone riding shotgun on top of the hay.

When we were several blocks from the barn where we were going to store the hay, Pete turned into the lane leading to the barn. As he turned, the load of hay did a slow lazy fall and scattered bales on the side of the lane.

We decided to unload the bales that remained on the truck and then return to get the ones on the ground.

We stored the bales that had stayed on the truck and then went back and picked up the ones on the ground. When I told Pete that I was right in not riding on top of the load, he almost agreed.

Pete's family moved when their dad bought a business in a larger town and sold most of his business properties in our town. He owned a gasoline station and a bulk station, and an oil product distribution center. The Catholic parish missed their generosity.

The hospital emergency room also missed them. The boys were regular customers for a variety of injuries, scrapes and fractures

SWIMMING IN A SANDPIT

In many stories there is a reference to the old swimming hole, a small town oasis revered in stories about boys swimming during the summer. Swimming holes were idealized to the point where readers of these stories considered them on a par with a municipal pool or club pool, but in any case, a safe, clean, and wholesome environment. This was not the case with ours.

Our swimming hole was on the north end of town not far from the *barrio.*

Several of us would occasionally go to an old sandpit, a place where our parents, needless to say, constantly warned us to stay away from. I heard many times about the dangers of "the sandpit," event though there were many around the outskirts of the town. The operating sandpits, that is, the ones where there was still sand being dredged for sale to construction companies and other users, were much cleaner than ours but a long ways away. All were south of town and we were at the north edge and didn't want to spend an hour walking to a sandpit where we couldn't swim anyway. I say our sandpit not because any of us owned it, but because we used it.

In groups of two or more, we went from the *barrio* to the swimming hole and swam. It wasn't exactly swimming.

We ran on the bank and executed a very shallow dive and returned to the bank as rapidly as possible. We took turns running and diving for about an hour, then dressed and returned home. We used the old sandpit for a couple of years but quit for good when we were finally allowed to enter the municipal swimming pool. Until that time, we were not allowed in the parks or the swimming pool.

We didn't realize it then, but swimming in the sandpit was clearly dangerous. We had been diving into murky water that covered old auto bodies and assorted junk. Any dive could have resulted in an evisceration of the diver if he dove too shallow and happened to rake his middle over a jagged edge.

One of my buddies, Satch, was a victim. He stepped on a piece of metal and punctured his foot. The wound was so large, he could barely walk home.

I don't know if he ever got a tetanus shot or tetanus itself but we stopped using the sandpit shortly after that.

Years later all this area was filled in and a plow manufacturing plant began operations.

The pool and the city parks were segregated for many years and it was not until the 1950s that the parks and pool were desegregated. The pool at the south end of town, the "colored pool" had been in use for as long as I can remember but it too was at the opposite end of town from the barrio.

VISITAS: ROLL YOUR OWN CIGARETTES

If there was sickness or death in the *barrio*, Doña Lola was there. Or so it seemed.

I think her profession was mourner on-call and visitor to the infirm, an apprentice Typhoid Mary sort of person. (There is no record of her in the local cemetery so she must be buried elsewhere.)

She was a large woman who wore the old type cotton hose usually rolled down, black skirts, peasant blouses and a spiffy hat. At least this was her visiting outfit. She may have dressed more or less elegantly at home, probably less since she lived in a converted railroad car.

By sickbeds and at funerals, Doña Lola was a picture of peace. At home, well, that's a different story to hear the neighbors tell it. They said she had a temper that was as short as her two daughters who regularly seemed to test it. If there was a husband and father in this family, he had disappeared before I was born.

According to the old folks, there were many occasions when neighbors reported loud noises and shouting coming from her house. This was usually followed by one or both of the daughters running from the house with their hands covering their heads and crying uncontrollably.

They said that it was not unusual to see Doña Lola chasing the daughters out of the house with a broomstick, a dishpan or other object harder than her daughters' heads.

Eventually, juvenile authorities placed the girls elsewhere based on various alleged transgressions.

Doña *Lola's* other trips into the neighborhood were to be with the other elderly women for a favorite pastime of roll-your-own cigarettes and conversation. The ingredients came from Prince Albert or Bull Durham tobacco and a foreign sounding cigarette paper.

The *barrio* women only smoked an occasional cigarette, never a store bought one and only with company at an afternoon *visita* or *soirée* as the French might call it.

I doubt that the smoking itself was as important as the assembling of the cigarettes. It was a social activity much like quilting. Virtually every little old lady in the *barrio* kept the "makings" in a shoebox or cigar box and brought out these "*fixins*" when company came to call. It took more time to get everyone ready to smoke than the time they actually smoked. It appeared to be a social status symbol more than a habit or addiction. In view of the time rolling and the constant relighting of the cigarettes, there was not much actual smoking although there was smoke, there was not much fire. I truly doubt that anyone ever inhaled.

On a bright summer afternoon with the sun shining through the lace curtains, one could see a bluish haze for hours after the smoking session. Second hand smoke was almost as plentiful as second hand clothes and previously owned furniture in the *barrio*.

Doña Lola died while I was still relatively young. (As mentioned previously, she is not buried in the local cemetery. Her daughters must have buried her elsewhere.)

DOÑA MARIQUITA

In today's terms she might be called anorexic as she was extremely thin and did not seem to eat much at all.

She was rumored to be of royal blood but so were the rest of us. She did look regal in the sense of a sixteenth century Spanish *señora*.

Her husband, Don Pancho, on the other hand, seemed to eat for both. She was a melancholy woman who was deathly afraid of tornadoes and should have lived elsewhere. Fargo, ND comes to mind since I have not heard of tornadoes there. She was born María Anchondo in 1880 and died in 1957. He was born Francisco Olivas in 1872 and died in 1949.

There was not much *joie de vivre*[20] in her household and an old radio was about her only communication with the outside world. This radio was a large piece of furniture and took up a significant amount of space in a rather small combination/multipurpose room that was a living room/parlor/dining room/bedroom. I mean it was small but functional.

The small house smelled of boiled cabbage and kerosene. Pinto beans do not have an overpowering aroma while cooking so other smells such as cabbage or *caldo de res* [21]overwhelmed the scent of beans cooking.

Kerosene was a fairly common smell around the more modern households in the *barrio*. The not so modern ones smelled of wood or coal smoke, barely indistinguishable from the air around the roundhouse up the road when the breeze was from the south.

Don Francisco, or Don Pancho, depending on who referred to him, was a Falstaff type character who was retired by the time I was old enough to toddle around. No one ever explained what he did before he retired. Many of us smaller kids thought he might have been a pirate or in later years when we started attending movies we imagined that he could have been a stand-in for Pancho Villa in the movies. He may have worked for the railroad but had no visible scars or disabilities to confirm the notion.

Don Pancho and Doña Mariquita were a psychology lesson in non-verbal communication. When they feuded, which seemed regularly, it was a sight to behold.

At the center of it all, was the radio. When he tuned the radio and sat down in his favorite chair, she would get up and change the station. This pattern continued silently with each alternating on changing the station. There was no local station at the time so who knows which stations they were tuning in. I admit that I never witnessed this personally but a very reliable party, my sister, did.

This routine would be broken only when a nephew who lived in El Paso, Texas came to visit and stayed for a week or two or for a couple of months.

DON PEDRO AND DOÑA MERCEDES

Perhaps, it was just old wives' tales or gossip that never seemed to end.

At any rate, the word of mouth in the *barrio* was that these neighbors were wizards, warlocks, or whatever type of magician one could conjure up, no pun intended.

Who was I not to join in the fun or one to try to stop the rumors?

Don Pedro and Doña Mercedes were colorful characters to say the least. Neither had worked outside the home since I had known them.

They managed to live on rental property income. They were among the landed gentry having two rental properties. Both properties were small one room houses (more modern terms would likely be "shacks" or "huts"), and these were rented all the time to the same two people.

One renter was a sweet old woman, Doña Felicitas, who harbored no ill will but did harbor about 30 cats of indistinct lineage.

An older single man, *El Güero*, a recipient of public assistance, who smoked funny cigarettes and decorated his one room in an eclectic manner not found anywhere today, occupied the other rental property.

He would have been well suited to reside in one of today's psychiatric nursing homes. The home's décor included the smell of smoke, urine and dried sweat, all of which had permeated the wallpaper of Civil War Surplus vintage. The place had an electric light, one electrical outlet but no running water, or for that matter, no running anything.

I think the *El Güero* was retired but I do not know from what. One summer evening he was hit by a car, while walking home. After his broken leg had healed, he spent most of his waking hours playing a drum, ostensibly practicing for a chair with the Matamoros (or perhaps, the *Matamoscas*[22]) Philharmonic.

He was a very light skinned Mexican but not as light as Vic. If there was musical talent in the family tree, it had not gotten to this branch.

He was an interesting storyteller but no one ever believed any of his tales of riding with Pancho Villa in *La Revolución*[23]. He claimed that he had been a *coronel*[24] in Villa's army, although from time to time he forgot and said that he was a *sargento*[25].

He told his tales to all the barrio kids that happened to walk by his home.

But back to Don Pedro and Doña Mercedes. They were reputed to conduct cabals or whatever term was in vogue in describing séances with the devil. No one really thought the devil lived in the barrio although it did seem hot enough at times.

If the devil had chosen to live there, s/he would have been better off financially than the rest of us. Don Pedro drove an old car with a bad clutch. The car and the clutch were both well worn out.

There were no new cars around the *barrio* and few even in town. During the war there were only a few available as the car manufacturers were manufacturing tanks and other war vehicles.

Don Pedro's car moved more or less of its own volition rather than at his command and control. The car itself was comparable to many of the other *carcanchas* in town but there were more of them in the more affluent black section of town.

Nights with a full moon were nights when we tried to avoid walking by this compound as devil worship sessions might, I stress might, be ongoing. No one ever saw any of these sessions but all were aware that they could be going on.

And one more thing: the cats, lots and lots of cats. And as everyone knows, cats have a lot to do with witches and devils. The fact that all the occupants of the property were good Catholics did nothing to dispel the rumors.

I always walked a little faster in this part of the alley on my way home after dark. While walking home from town or anywhere else, it was necessary to either walk down the alley by this area or walk along the highway. The highway was dangerous and had no street lights so there was nothing to gain by walking there as opposed to walking in the alley.

The stories—I mean rumors—lived long after the couple's death. (I found no grave marker for them on my last trip to the local cemetery so have no firm dates of birth or death.)

Don Teófilo

Don Teófilo Saenz was born, according to his grave marker, 12/25/1883 and died 1/14/1968. He had literally gone to the dogs by the time I knew him, or perhaps, the dogs had actually gone to him.

He lived in one of the one-room hovels in the compound up the alley from Don P and kept at least 15 dogs of unknown ancestry. He bought fresh Danish rolls from the Dillon's bakery and milk for the dogs. He did not eat any of this himself.

His diet was pretty much the basic food groups that we all enjoyed--chile, beans, tortillas and seasonal vegetables. He also smoked funny cigarettes and drove a *carcancha* with a lousy clutch and dog poop on the seats and what remained of the upholstery.

Until he died many years ago, he provided unpaid taxi service for the family up the alley that reportedly was related to him. I say reportedly because there was no family resemblance nor talk about any relationship.

Unlike that family, he was a gentle person. In comparison to the bellicose family, the resident bullies, he was a saint. Although he professed to be Roman Catholic, he never went near the church.

The recipients of his taxi service weren't Catholic or any other denomination but did attend revival services whenever they occurred in the barrio. The scene of these spiritual makeovers was up the alley two houses away.

A self-styled evangelist, an elderly woman with gray hair fixed in a bun and wearing a plain cotton dress, preached in a one-room mission whenever the spirit moved her. Her husband always brought along his aged violin upon which he screeched out a hymn or two and scared the devil out of those in attendance.

In later years, all of these folks disappeared and probably died sometime while I was away. In any event there were no services in the mission building after 1955 to my knowledge.

The organ in the mission disappeared sometime in 1956, perhaps the work of the usual suspects in the *barrio*. No one knows to this day whether it was sold or for how much. Organs, even the small ones are heavy and awkward to move so maybe a professional mover handled the move and it went to a church with a poor congregation, or maybe even a museum somewhere. It was an old organ with German names on the small brass plate above the keyboard.

The old violin was worth more than it appeared to be worth and was autographed by a famous violinist who once played a concert in the town. I believe the violinist's name was Joseph Szigeti or something close to that.

According to rumors, the violin too disappeared later on and may have appeared in a pawn shop in one of the larger cities nearby.

Eventually the one room mission church disappeared, torn down or burned down, I have not yet found out what actually happened. One day it was there then 20 years later it wasn't. By the time it disappeared, there was no preacher to conduct services, nor anyone to attend.

SOME WHITE FOLKS

Tom, one of the few white folks in the barrio, owned a team of large black horses. With the horses he moved houses, plowed gardens and hauled stuff on his wagon. One of his sons drank and two did not, but all were strange in their own way.

One of the sons was a lumberjack and visited occasionally from his home in the forests of Oregon. Another lived in town but worked out of town a lot and neither one spent much time at home or tending the horses.

When Tom's wife Minnie died, he sold the house and, I think, died shortly thereafter. My uncle "Eppy" bought the house and modernized it.

Son number three, *el Chale*, was a singular case. He worked on the railroad, a real job, and had strange mannerisms. For instance, he laughed hilariously at jokes or situations but not a sound emanated from his mouth, even though his body was contorted with laughter.

His wife was a little strange too but smoked heavily and eventually died of lung problems. He was born in 1912 and died in 1987 she was born in 1917 and died in 1995. She kept her house immaculately clean. I was only there on a couple of occasions to invite them to our house for a picnic or other function.

My sister hung out there a lot with their daughter, her close friend. They played together often.

Despite her mother's dislike of Mexican folks generally and several specifically, the daughter married one of the local guys. Even without benefit of a high school diploma, he landed a good-paying job at the

Boeing plant in Wichita. He retired after suffering a stroke. She did not finish high school, possibly because she never attended.

El Chale suffered a heart attack or stroke then took a disability retirement from the railroad and did virtually nothing for his remaining years. He had worked on the section gang with my dad and was accustomed to hard labor but really slowed down after the physical disaster.

For as long as he lived, *Chale* continued to wear clean starched overalls. He painted his house once so his disability retirement years were not totally wasted.

El Chale did not garden, did not smoke, and did not play a musical instrument. He drank a great deal of cider and coffee.

LOS PÉRSICOS[26]

A poor white family with around seven kids--there may have been more, no outsider had an accurate count-- lived out in the middle of a wheat field about a quarter mile from the nearest *barrio* abode. Some of the neighbors called them Los Pérsicos because they couldn't pronounce their last name which was Pattinson, Patterson, Peterson or some combination of letters with a similar pronunciation.

Their garage, an old tin shed, or at least a wooden framed structure covered with thin metal on the outside, served as a pigeon coop. It had a trapdoor where unwary pigeons would land to peck at the corn on the shelf and fall into the garage as the shelf flopped them in.

The kids attended school mostly in the fall while the weather was nicer. It was a long walk to the North School and there was no one at home to push them to attend in bad weather or at any time. They hardly ever finished the school year.

Years later, one of the sons did return to school. Unfortunately it was the state reformatory for boys where he was sent for a three-year term. He was one of three *barrio* citizens to serve time, but the only white one up to that time.

Another convicted evildoer was the younger son of the family two doors south of our home. He held up a filling station one summer evening and hit the old man working there on the head with a wrench. The old guy was the father of one of my high school classmates.

For this robbery he did time in the reformatory and was lucky to be tried as a juvenile rather than as an adult. The third person to serve time in the reformatory was a black kid from one of two black families that lived in the *barrio*. Prison was an equal opportunity institution.

The father of the *Pérsicos* worked for the railroad in one of the higher paying jobs. He had obtained the job of fireman with the assistance of his brother-in-law, also a fireman and 32nd degree Mason. Despite the high pay and opportunity to become a locomotive engineer, he opted to quit the railroad and do farm work such as driving a truck to the elevator during the wheat harvest, driving a tractor to plow and other chores around the farm. This career was dead-ended but this did not seem to matter much to him. The pay cut must have been enormous as farm hands were paid very low wages while firemen earned hefty paychecks.

None of the other adult males in the family were known to work on a farm or anywhere else. The rest of the family seemed to spend their time figuring out how to get money without working. The oldest daughter married a young man who had a job. It was an event that raised the social status of the family.

Misfortune struck the family who joined the ranks of the homeless when their house burned down one summer afternoon. The family was forced to save what they could which was not a whole lot except for a few clothes. After this disaster, they moved closer to the other houses in the *barrio*. They were able to buy a couple of lots at the far north end of the *barrio* in what was previously a wheat field and they eventually built a house on the property. Until the house was finished they lived with relatives and in a trailer that they must have borrowed from someone. No one could figure out how a family so poor and devastated by fire could afford to start anew without money since, as previously stated, none of them seemed to work.

Eventually one of the older sons went to work in the oilfields as a roughneck, an occupation not a skin condition. The pay was good but he did not stick with it for more than a year and a few months. He claimed that his back was bad, a condition that certainly was possible given the heavy lifting required on the job. After he quit, drilling for oil dropped off and many other roughnecks were out of work. From more than 25 drilling rigs working in the immediate area, the number of active rigs dropped to fewer than six.

The family acquired two horses after their house was finished and they had moved in. No one knew how the family could afford horses on their income. They knew very little about caring for horses and failed to take proper care of them. The horses deteriorated into poor health and looked shabby.

One summer day a younger son, JL, who was also known as "Shakey," went to the library riding one of the horses, a dark horse named *Baldy*. The nickname *Shakey* evolved from his initials, JL, which were coalesced into *Jake, Jakey, Chakey* and finally " *Shakey*".

The library event was noticed by the local press and a reporter, perhaps the only local reporter, took a picture and wrote a brief article about modes of transportation to the summer reading program. No one bothered to ask the rider if he could read but the effort was valiant, and it did provide a human-interest story. There was even a follow-up story that centered on the horse.

In the article, the reporter pointed out the horse's hooves were all chopped up and uneven and that the horse walked funny. Upon closer inspection, he saw that the hooves appeared to be chiseled and not trimmed evenly. In an interview with the reporter, the spokesperson for the family, the father, confirmed that he had indeed trimmed the horse's hooves with a cold chisel since he had no rasps, hoof knives or other gear to properly trim hooves. He did know about hoof knives but had never owned or used one.

Luckily, a local horse owner, who did know how to trim horses' hooves, offered to trim both horses' hooves after reading the article in the paper and seeing the pictures of the botched job that the owner had done. As was customary, several of the neighborhood kids gathered to watch this delicate operation. Afterwards, the horses continued to walk somewhat funny until they adjusted to having level hooves and got their leg muscles accustomed. After a couple of weeks, they no longer rocked slightly but rather just walked in a proper horse like manner.

JOHN DEERE TRACTOR

I remember vividly an event that involved a member of this family and an old John Deere tractor. Even in this era, most modern tractors had pneumatic tires (those made of rubber and filled with air) and controls such as gears, clutches, and brakes.

One late spring day, one of the older members of the family, a male, there was only one female in the family, came chugging down the alley on an old tractor with steel wheels. The wheels had spikes or lugs, metal pieces four or so inches across and about three inches high. There were many spikes so the tractor left a noticeable path carved into the earth.

My younger brother, Manuel, and I followed this tractor up the unpaved street that led to their old family homestead. When we got there, we talked to the driver who said that he was there to plow a garden near where the family home had burned. But just then, he put up his hands and proclaimed, "Can't do it." That was no surprise to us. He had no plow. The family finally hired Tom and his team of horses to plow them a garden plot.

A LARGE MIGRANT FAMILY

On occasions, migrants came through town and gravitated to the north end. Two migrants lived in our caboose for a month or two and finally moved on to western Kansas where work was more plentiful. There were migrants who lived year round in the *barrio* but traveled west to work on large farms during the seasons when there was work for them

Don Camilo was not related to anyone else in the barrio other than his own large family. The family was engaged in migrant labor, traveling to western Kansas for the seasonal work. The family worked broomcorn, sugar beets and the weeding, thinning and harvesting of other vegetables. This labor was hard, hot and not highly paid but with several family members working, did yield a living.

From the time that the children were six or otherwise able to fend for themselves, they were expected to contribute in some way to the family income. For the smaller children, it might mean taking care of themselves while the older ones worked in the fields. The older ones who worked in the fields did not see any future in going to school, so when they were in town, they did not attend school for very long in those years when they were actually enrolled. There was no tuition charged at the Catholic School so there was no financial commitment to the school by those kids who were enrolled, consequently many did not attend.

Doña María R was a housewife by profession. If she had had a choice, she would likely have ended child bearing at three rather than seven or however many there actually were. Her two oldest daughters spent a lot of time working at home and one eventually worked as a chambermaid at the local hotel during the winter when the family was in town and not out in the fields. This daughter was an attractive young woman, who eventually married a migrant man and they moved to another town. Her older sister hardly ever left the house and never married. There may be a cause and effect situation here.

All the sons worked at migrant labor at some point in their life. One of the older ones joined the army and learned a skill, as well as better English. He later obtained a government job upon returning from the Army. On one of his visits home, he said that he had many army experiences that served him well in later life. He was a success story for the family.

The three youngest brothers did not fare so well. They continued to live at home, slopping the hogs, milking the cow and doing day labor. All three are currently disabled and not working even though they are only in their mid to late 50s. None of the three went to school beyond the third grade and while in town, and attended the Catholic School sparingly at best.

The oldest son, Juan, was a quick learner. He spoke English well although he did not attend school much more than the others. He learned to play the violin and the mandolin on his own.

Musical trivia. (When I told my father, a master musician, about Juan's talent, he pointed out that the strings are the same on both the mandolin and the violin: G, D, A, and E. My father told me that the fingering also is basically the same but the violin does not have frets and uses a bow to evoke the sound while the mandolin is plucked with a pick.)

Unfortunately, his interest and talent in fixing cars led to his death. One summer day, he was priming the carburetor on his neighbor's car by pouring gasoline into the carburetor. When the engine finally started, it backfired shooting a flame upward from the carburetor and showering him with burning gasoline.

Several witnesses went into shock and did not know what to do, so did little, actually nothing. Finally someone standing nearby threw cold water on him which did not put out the fire. This was not the proper thing to do, but no one knew anything about smothering gasoline fires. He died on the way to the hospital.

If someone had known to smother the flames with a blanket or something else, he might have survived. He was born in1930 and died in 1944. Although five years older, he was a good friend with whom I could talk and hang around. He was a kind, bright kid, a rarity in those days. A boy born into the family about twelve years later was named Juan after the deceased.

Don Camilo ultimately landed a section hand job on the railroad and settled out of the migrant stream. While working for the railroad, he still managed a small farm, that some would call a garden but he also raised pigs and a cow which he milked daily, so I guess he did have a farm.

Like his son Juan, he too played the violin although not as well and hardly ever gathered a crowd to listen. His sons usually left the house when he took out the violin. Most of those who actually heard his renditions of violin music did so in transit. If we happened to walk by his house while he sat on the back porch and played, we heard him playing. I do not recall that any listener actually identified any piece that he played or that anyone made a real effort to stop to listen to the impromptu concert. We always waved hello and kept going.

Whether our inability to properly identify his music was due to our own limited knowledge of the classics or to his rendition of whatever he attempted to play, will never be known. He had a very extensive collection of Beto Villa records, but none of the polkas or other pieces seemed to influence him enough to learn to play any of them. He was a hardy soul and accustomed to hard labor.

Some of the things that I noticed about him were the thick calloused hands, the fruits of his work as a migrant laborer. His career on the railroad and his work around his house did nothing to lessen the coarseness of his hands. I'm sure that he could have handled most anything without gloves and never suffered pain while doing so.

He butchered a hog at least once a year. It was interesting to watch how he accomplished this task. Before he or one of the older sons killed the hog, the other sons had started to boil water in a 55-gallon drum over an open fire. After the hog bled out, the next step in preparing the carcass was not the skinning but rather the shaving of the hair off the hide. With the boiling water, they scalded the hog and the hair came off much more easily. Only after the hair was all shaved off did they begin cutting up the carcass.

The crew eviscerated the hog saving the liver as well as other internal organs. The remaining "stuff" was recycled to the garden or, perhaps, to other pigs as feed. The hog was quartered so that the individual pieces would not be too heavy to cut up further. Much of the meat was left with the skin on to be further cut up later. Most of the pieces that had deep fat layers were rendered for the lard and the skin portion was then cooked yielding *chicharones*.

I do not recall this family buying meat at the store or having to purchase lard. Some of the pieces were dried and saved for later and some meat was prepared as *carne adobada*[27] that is, marinated for many hours with a sauce of ground red chile and secret family spices and then cooked and eaten or dried and saved for later consumption.

María had the distinction of being the only female ever to attend the "Farmers & Merchants Stag," a male only party staged annually by the town businessmen. These local merchants sponsored the evening by providing ham & beans and the trimmings for the invited guests, which meant anyone who could read the invitation in the local newspaper. The tickets were free and available at most downtown stores. Since Doña

María couldn't read English, or other languages, she ended up at the stag party after hearing about it from her sons who had picked up tickets at one of the local gas stations.

I'm not sure she ever realized why other women did not attend.

She later remarked that the food was good but that the boxing matches were not. Boxing was always the evening's entertainment. Her presence was noted by an avid reporter for the local paper who managed to eke out an article about the event.

In this town it was not remarkable that the whole family was there, only that the lady of the house had also attended. Perhaps none of them could read English well enough to know what "stag" meant.

A few years ago Don Camilo died at age 94, a much older age than several of his children who had died in their 60s. His grave marker shows his birth date as 8/18/1904, died 9/14/1998. Doña María was born 9/1/1904, died 7/3/1979. Other family members are still alive and living in the area but not in the *barrio.*

Some members of the family had rather strange nicknames. There was *Chon,* short for Asención, *Cuco,* short for Refugio and *Shorty*, short for stature. Refugio is no longer a popular name and even at this time, few persons carry this name.

Cuco suffered from other *apodos* when some of the nastier kids called him *"Refugee", "Cuckoo"* and other less flattering names. Despite this disrespect, he was the family member who left and had a successful adulthood in the government job previously mentioned.

There are still a few older folks called *Cuco* or *Cuca,* the feminine form, but these Old World names are given very sparingly today. In an era when 90 percent of the women were named "María de something", ranging from *La Concepción* to *El Pilar* or *Lourdes,* these women were generally called by the second part of the name, such as, Pilar, Lourdes or Dolores.

BENNIE GETS NAILED

Since most, if not all the houses in the barrio burned wood, chopping wood was a mandatory pastime.

This was and maybe still is a boy's job. In 1940s girls did housework, not "heavy lifting" type work outdoors. Boys by gender and tradition chopped wood. Even widows who lived alone did not have to chop their own wood. If she were a madrina to a husky lad, he would usually chop wood for her on a fairly regular basis. Scrap lumber was a major source of firewood but required cutting the longer pieces down to stove size.

Scrap lumber contained nails, which were removed by hand with a hammer and sometimes a nail puller, a special tool for removing nails. Woodpiles were just that--jumbled piles of wood. These woodpiles almost always had boards with nails and these were usually underneath the cleaner boards. In addition to nails, there were splinters and other dangerous items in the woodpile that would attack the unwary woodchopper.

Bennie had the misfortune to be the designated woodchopper for the family one Saturday afternoon on a cool spring day. As the stack of cut firewood grew, the pile of scrap diminished.

There were only a few more boards left on the ground when Bennie stepped on one of them but slipped sideways and came down on one with a nail sticking up. The nail penetrated his right heel and ended the wood chopping session. He hobbled into the kitchen and told his mom what had just happened.

In accord with the prevalent notion on what to do after stepping on a nail, his mom cleaned the wound and put a piece of tape on his heel. Others might have worried about "lockjaw" and sought a Tetanus shot. Only a hospital or a doctor's office could provide a Tetanus shot, so few folks ever got one.

As expected, Bennie's wound got infected. By the time he received medical treatment, doctors had to remove the infected portion of his heel. Unfortunately, Bennie limped badly for the rest of his life. To make up for the missing portion of heel, he slanted his body in the direction of the smaller heel.

Bennie died in his mid 40s, a victim of perhaps of early childhood injuries or other factors but the amputation of part of his heel and the aftermath of the infection certainly contributed to his shortened life. In his case, an ounce of prevention could have prevented a ton of pain.

Even after this episode, few barrio folks thought seriously about Tetanus shots or medical attention for wounds from rusty nails or other metal objects. Most folks were aware of the dangers of infection. They still nevertheless relied on old remedies to protect them from infection, amputation and death.

DON JOSÉ AND DOÑA ROSA

I have always pictured Don José and Doña Rosa on the cover of Better Homes and Gardens magazine.

Of course, it could never have happened.

There was no way that a national magazine would ever come to the *barrio*. Or any reason why the magazine editors would even think of it. I don't think Kansas was ever on their map, let alone Pratt or our *barrio*.

Today, sixty plus years later, there might be a chance with Latinos now making up a significant part--not only in the general population but in the billion dollar economy--that some fingers might snap in the mind of a New York editor and exclaim, "What about a story on a nice Latino family."

Just a thought.

If ever there was a model for a man with a green thumb, it was Don José.

He did gardening for the rich folks in town, all of whom tried to contract him exclusively early in the year. He refused to be tied to any one family or person but preferred to work for several people.

His gardening work was a source of pride for those whom he chose to work for and the envy of those who didn't get on his work schedule.

Since he was a diabetic, he was not supposed to drink beer. He abided by that religiously. Soft drinks, well, that was another matter. He drained a 12 ounce bottle of soft drink in one gulp. Other than in modern time television commercials, I have never seen anyone else actually do this.

His work was the envy of anyone who thought they had talent in landscaping. He could green up lawns in the spring that stayed green all through the hottest summers. His artistry in trimming bushes was remarkable. He could have passed on his knowledge to his sons or daughters but unfortunately there were none.

In today's world he could teach courses at a community college and earn a decent amount of money. This would not interfere with his day job since many of this type of courses are night classes.

He drove an old pickup truck until his eyesight proved too feeble to enable him to renew his license. Bad knees then caught up with him. He and his wife quit going to Sacred Heart Church except when some neighbors offered them a ride. On some Saturdays, the priest would administer the sacrament of Holy Communion at home.

In his 60s, Don José got a leg infection. The doctor ordered him to the hospital to amputate his right leg that had been diagnosed as gangrenous.

Don José vehemently opposed it. "Sorry, doctor, I'm going home. If I die, I want to die with all of my limbs still attached to my body."

When Don José came home, Doña Mercedes took over with her knowledge of herbs—not the witchcraft that was the talk of the *barrio*. The word in the *barrio* was that she mixed a poultice of beet tops (leaves) with secret herbs and other ingredients which were soaked in water and applied three times daily. There were other substances in the mix but only the leaves were visible.

After a few days the infection *not only stopped spreading* but also actually *started receding*.

Miracle of miracles, in just over a month there were no signs of the infection. Don José lived several more years. But the saving of his leg was not sufficient to extend his master gardening.

Just as Don José was renowned for his gardening skills, his wife, Doña Rosa was famous in the *barrio* for her meticulous housekeeping. Her house was immaculate both inside and outside. She planted and raised various flowers. While I can't vouch for the names of the flowers, I still recall vividly the aromas. To this day I have not smelled flowers such as those she had in the garden and in her house.

They had no children of their own but were friendly to all the *barrio* kids. They always had treats for us for Halloween and at Christmas time. There was a custom in the *barrio* that kids would visit neighbors on Christmas Eve and receive treats. I know of no other place where this custom is or was practiced. It may have been a variation of *Las Posadas*[28].

This popular couple died several years apart. He preceded her in death. I've always thought the couple could have been models for a magazine article on long lasting marriage as well as meticulous habits. I remember them fondly and think about them when I visit the cemetery. (She was born María on 9/1/1888 died 6/23/1970. He, José Martínez, was born on 12/10/1886, died 1963. Both are buried in the local cemetery.)

TINKERS AND TAILORS

Don Aristeo—now that's a name that hasn't found its way into modern times--was a tailor who could take a piece of cloth and fashion a luxurious garment out of it at a nominal price.

Despite the price, no one in the barrio could afford his services so he worked for the upper crust of society in the town. He cut and sewed suits, gowns, dresses and other garments, I guess, although I never saw any.

He spent time in the *barrio* in Kansas and the majority of his time in the interior of Mexico. His home was a village in the Mexican state of Oaxaca. The village had an Indian name with around five consonants and only two vowels. His wife never came to the US, and he never became a naturalized citizen although he was a semi-permanent resident.

Tony the tailor, as he was called, learned enough English to work, but not enough to study much of anything in the town or to even read much more than the daily newspaper. Many of his evenings were spent reading books in Spanish.

He could maneuver through patterns and order forms but with difficulty. He lived frugally and sent most of his money to his family in Mexico. He kept enough to live on and even enough to buy a car. The dollar went further in Mexico than in Kansas. Although he was a tailor, he never wore flashy clothes and looked a lot like the other denizens of the *barrio*.

He drove a car that was spotless, at least in contrast to other cars in the neighborhood. Rumor had it that he was related to folks in the neighborhood, Don Pancho and Doña Mariquita, although no one ever figured out the relationship and neither he nor they ever mentioned it. Given the tranquil life in the region of Mexico where he lived, he probably lived many more years after leaving the US. No one heard from him after he left in the mid 1950s following news that his daughter had died at a young age.

THE CIRCUS IS IN TOWN

Circuses came through town during the summer and were stellar attractions in small towns. Today's circuses set up in arenas and generally stay for several days. Back then, circuses were small and stayed for only two performances in each town.

We lived in the county seat and smaller towns could not attract circuses so these rural citizens usually came to our town to attend the circus.

One summer day a man wearing a suit showed up at the house and inquired whether we owned the garage that faced the corner of the alley and the street. When he had verified that it indeed was ours, he asked if he could put a large circus poster on the north wall.

For displaying the poster, he would give us two complimentary tickets to the circus performance. We planned to go anyway so two free tickets for the evening performance would be very welcome. The poster on the garage was about 10-by-18 feet and covered the whole wall. This was about a month before the circus was due in town. There weren't many people that drove by our garage so we did not think that a whole lot of people would see our poster.

The poster itself had pictures of several wild animals, tigers, lions, elephants and camels. Most of the barrio kids walked by our garage several times a day to admire the poster that looked like a mural. The poster lasted almost the whole winter but the heavy snows that year wiped it out by April.

One of the highlights of the circus that year was that we got to see the unloading of the animals. It was a two-hour show for us. The circus train had around 30 cars including equipment cars, passenger cars where the performers and roustabouts lived during the season and flatcars with cages for the animals.

Roustabouts were the people who worked around the circus but were not necessarily professional performers. They put up the tent, fed the animals, and performed many chores that were necessary to keep everything in proper order for the performances.

That year the parade made it through town, including our Main Street, which was fairly long, and the depot area, which was around 10 blocks from the business district.

The parade proceeded from the tracks south through the business district. Those who lived along Main Street could watch the parade from their front porch. All others watched the parade from the sidewalks along the street. The parade turned around after going through the business district which ran from First Street to Fifth Street. The parade returned to the circus area via a side street then back on Main Street past Fourth Street and First Street.

The concession tents and stalls were set up in time for the afternoon performance when all the animals were ready and poised to perform. Tigers and lions usually appeared in one act in the center ring and everybody gasped when the fearless animal trainer stuck his head in a lion's mouth. Bears rode bicycles, seals caught balls on their noses, and horses pranced around the ring with scantily clad women standing on their backs. Camels never did much other than walking in the parade and having a young woman in a harem costume leading them around the ring.

Elephants did the talent part of the program. They stood on their head, rolled huge balls around the ring, ran around trunk to tail, and hoisted other young women up on their heads with their trunks. A more daring stunt was having a huge elephant place a front foot on the trainer's face while he was flat on the ground.

The evening performance was shorter as the circus had to load everything on the train and travel to their next town. Typically, the evening performance ended with the elephants following the crowd toward the exit. This tended to clear the tent fairly fast.

This era was long before there was television, but the performances were live. In addition, we also had an occasional medicine show.

The circuses were primarily smaller ones with three rings. The larger circuses appeared in larger cities such as Topeka, Wichita and Kansas City. We got to see the likes of Cole Brothers Circus, which was a smaller one but still pretty good.

One particular circus that I remember from an even earlier age came to town in July. A neighbor, who lived up the alley, and I decided to go work at the circus and earn some money. We were both around 10 years old at the time and had more aspirations than ability.

We arrived at the vacant lot where the circus set up and looked around for someone to hire us for something.

Only an old Gypsy woman, who claimed to speak Spanish, Italian, French and other languages, hired us to bring water in an ancient milk can. She said she couldn't pay us money but she would tell our fortune.

We took the milk can and went to our windmill and filled the can with cool fresh water. We struggled with the heavy can but got it back to her. She read our palm and told us good things would happen to us.

My neighbor later went to prison so she was not too accurate with his long range fortune.

Another memorable circus came to town on the day that my sister Dolores and I were scheduled to have our tonsils and adenoids removed. We were unable to attend the circus and felt badly about it until a couple of years ago after carrying a grudge for 50 plus years.

We finally rationalized that the circus wasn't all that great so we really didn't miss much. In modern times we could have seen the circus acts on television even in the hospital.

THE MEDICINE SHOW

Yet another source of entertainment was the "Medicine Show".

I have not been to one in over 60 years and I doubt that there are any in existence today.

At that time, at least one medicine show came to town, always in the summer and always with a portable stage with a tent roof.

One that I remember better than others was the "Keenetone Medicine Show" which came around three or four times between 1945 and 1949.

The show's master of ceremonies was "Flapjacks," a clown, magician and public speaker. He may have been a preacher in the off season but he never mentioned what his real job was.

The cast put on short plays with costumes and props. One of their favorites was "South Dakota Widow." I don't remember the plot, only the title. I had no idea what or where South Dakota was until years later. The main purpose of the medicine show was to sell the product line.

Flapjacks exhorted the audience to buy their great products that ranged from tooth powder, (not powdered teeth but rather powder for brushing teeth) to corn plasters. He also sold toothache medicine, and some kind of balm to rub on sunburn, scars, and moles.

He was shrewd. He made no promises about healing anything. He just said buy it and use it. He also sold candy in small boxes that he guaranteed to contain a prize if you bought a whole row of boxes, eight for a dollar.

I recall that on a couple of occasions, we did buy a dollar's worth and found coupons for very nice prizes including a carving set consisting of a large fork and large very sharp knife.

Other prizes were grooming sets, which included a small hand mirror, a comb and a brush. On the last night of the medicine show's run in each town, they had a talent show. Many of the local kids, the more courageous ones, competed.

My sister was one of the brave ones who competed. Although she did not win, she did place second. She lost to one of my kindergarten classmates. He was a tenor and sang a gushy song that the audience liked. She played a classical piece on the piano and no one in the audience had heard it before or really cared that is was extremely difficult to play.

RIDING IN A PARADE FLOAT

One Saturday, month and year forgotten, a tall white woman appeared at our old house and asked my parents if we, the kids, could participate in a parade by riding on a float. I was about eight. The float was actually an old pick up truck with stock rails on the sides. It probably was used to haul cattle on weekdays but that day it would haul kids.

The gist of the parade was to influence voters to vote against allowing the sale of liquor. Kansas had been a "dry" state for many years, probably since the days of prohibition or maybe always.

The float may have been sponsored by the Women's Christian Temperance Union (WCTU) or perhaps some other anti-liquor group.

There were cardboard signs on the sides of the truck with statements such as "The children of the world need grain for food." How the use of grain for food elsewhere interfered with or was negatively affected by using grain for liquor never got through to us but the women in charge seemed to think they had a clear message for the immediate world. Another sign that I remember was "This dry rot we hear about is a lot of Tommyrot'. I did not know what it meant then and it is of no consequence now.

There were other signs arguing against the "open saloon" which, they claimed had been outlawed by the Kansas constitution many years prior to that date. Up to this date the only alcoholic beverage sold in Kansas was 3.2 percent alcohol beer.

Wealthy citizens could consume strong liquor at the country club or other private clubs but not over the bar at public places. The farce of prohibition was still in effect for most citizens except the chosen few who could afford the private club approach. Poorer folks could purchase and consume beer or, if they knew someone who could obtain "hard liquor," could purchase whiskey.

Despite all the signs and pleas by the anti liquor groups, the election went against them and the county voted to allow liquor sales in package stores. Bars continued serving 3.2 percent beer but no hard liquor. Private clubs continued to operate but could sell liquor over the bar instead of having individual bottles for members, which they could store in their lockers or on the shelf at the bar.

Arrests for drunken driving did not increase nor did the incidence of public drunkenness. Public life concerning drinking did not appear to change after the legalization of liquor sales. Previously rich folks were not arrested for driving while drinking. They were usually escorted home, as the police knew them to be pillars of the community who had a drinking problem but were otherwise harmless.

Poorer folks drank at home since they did not belong to private clubs and thus did not have to drive anywhere. Weekend drinking did not require driving anywhere after morning church services.

We never learned how the children of the world fared without the grain used by the liquor industry.

BOY SCOUTS AT WORK

There was a time when Armistice Day was a real celebration in November—not the Veterans Day of today's celebrations.

I remember it well, for it offered 13 members of my Boy Scout Troop and me a chance to earn $25.00.

For the $25.00, our troop, Number 129, sponsored by Sacred Heart Catholic Church, was asked to help direct traffic for the Armistice Day parade. On this occasion we were all dressed in our make shift uniforms, not official since ours were of khaki clothes and not the official greenish color of Boy Scout uniforms.

All 14 of us walked up and down the curbs along Main Street and asked people to:

"Please step up to the sidewalk. The parade is coming."

Our friends and neighbors laughed at us and scorned us as we performed our task of crowd control. They did manage to follow our instructions but not willingly, quickly or jovially.

At this time, there were several scout troops in town and Sacred Heart, the only Catholic Church in town, or the two Methodist and one Baptist Churches sponsored all troops. The protestant troops were much better financed than ours.

With our windfall money, we purchased a war surplus pyramid tent for camping. Unfortunately, we found out that it was not as waterproof as advertised.

El Caballo Blanco

One fine summer day, a large white horse materialized in the barrio.

The horse was wandering in the alley and not really bothering anyone, but everyone who saw him was afraid. The horse was big and did not look friendly. The blood his chest added to the dangerous look.

We all knew that all the horses in Mr. Tom's stable were black and even though they too were large, they were gentle and around people all the time. They plowed gardens, moved houses and did other draft work as they were draft horses but of no particular breed. They were not purebred anything but were just good workhorses. They may have been specimens of a noteworthy breed but no one at that time knew anything about Belgians, Clydesdales or Percherons. What I now know is that the horses were none of these.

A small crowd, mostly women and youth, gathered after the mysterious white horse ambled into Tom's stable yard and settled in to munch on the hay that was always available there.

Within several minutes, the neighborhood team trotted down the alley toward the stable yard. When they arrived, the assembled multitude greeted Tom with the news that a large wild horse was in his stable yard and appeared bloody. This was quite obvious to him, and the immediate world, but all present felt compelled to pass on the information.

Several theories came forth at the top of shrill female voices such as:

"He looks like he's been fighting;"

"That poor horse is wounded;"

"Someone hurt him and he ran away;" and,

"He got cut trying to get away from his cruel master."

(Apparently those in the crowd had forgotten or did not remember how Tom previously treated his team of mules. Most of the older residents remarked often that he regularly beat the mules with a 2-by-4 or whatever was handy. Since the mules had long ago been sold, rendered for soap or otherwise disposed of, no one had fresh memories of the cruel master that Tom had allegedly been.)

No one wanted to help catch the horse nor to even get close. The horse looked formidable with his broad white chest dripping blood across a narrow horizontal line that marked his whole front.

Tom, much more familiar with horses than anyone else, simply walked up to the horse while talking to him, put his arm around the horse's neck, put a halter on him, and led him to the stable. This, of course, was long before the "Horse Whisperer Approach" became more widely known.

Tom explained that the horse probably went through a barbed wire fence and got a slight cut on his chest where the top wire hit him and that he was very lucky to not get tangled in the lower strands. He could have sawed off a hoof or seriously injured himself, in which case, he would not have mysteriously appeared in the neighborhood as he would have been unable to walk and would, consequently, have been put down.

Within a couple of days of this event, there appeared an ad in the local paper in the "Lost, Strayed or Stolen" column that described the horse and offered a small reward for his return. By the time the owner came to reclaim his horse, the horse was reluctant to leave. Finally the owner enticed him into a trailer with hay and carrots.

The horse probably thought he had it pretty easy, not having to work and a manger always full of hay.

THE DAY THE COWS CAME HOME ALONE

On an afternoon in early fall when the sun was still warm and comfortable, farmer Tom looked out the window and was surprised to see four of his cows walking home--unescorted.

What was missing was his farmhand, David, who took care of the cows and did other odd jobs. This is not to say that looking after cows is an odd job, only that odd jobs was a catchall category of chores that required little or no formal education.

After all, there is no Bachelor of Science degree in cow herding, or is there?

Alarmed that his farmhand, who was quite old, might be injured, Tom dashed out of the house. As Tom later told the story, he knew exactly where to search.

"I just kept looking for the smoke, and sure enough, I found David smoking a roll-your-own-cigarette," he said. It was probably Bull Durham, since this would be more appropriate to smoke while watching the cows.

David later told anyone who was willing to hear his story that while walking the four cows toward home from greener pastures; literally, he tripped on a tree branch and fell. The cows continued on their way home, which they knew by heart or smell as the case may be.

Most of us were used to seeing David with his arms over a cow's neck, one under each arm, as the convoy came home. Unescorted cows, while not a rarity, were not a daily occurrence either. Tom, fearing the worst, backtracked to where the cows had been pasturing, and a quarter mile or so back, found David on the ground in obvious pain.

He told Tom that when he tripped on the tree branch, he tried to turn so as to hit on a softer and more shock absorbent part of his anatomy and in doing so, had turned an ankle such that he could not walk. Hoping that someone would find him before dark, he had waited patiently smoking a cigarette.

HOUSE MOVING AND OTHER EVENTS

Tom did many jobs with his team of black draft horses, including things that the original teamsters, reportedly, used to do. One of these jobs was to move houses.

Don Mónico, who wanted his house moved across two lots onto a foundation that he had constructed on his new property, hired him.

The house was constructed of leftover lumber from railroad construction jobs. The new property was across the alley from our family compound. Tom and his horses showed up early while it was relatively cool, and the team was ready for the pull as were many of the *barrio* kids who had gotten up early on a Saturday to watch the event. Several of us climbed onto the roof of one of the sheds in our backyard where we could have a better view.

Tom hitched the team up to the house which he had jacked up and placed on trucks that had large pneumatic tires (previous note on inflatable tires). It took a few minutes to get everything ready. Finally with a mighty heave the team started the pull. Difficult at the start, the pull seemed easier as they moved along.

Were it not for the neighborhood kids to witness this historic event, it might have gone largely unnoticed. There was no press coverage.

Once the pull started, the trip took about 30 minutes and generated a lot of sweat on the horses, the driver and the spectators. The distance involved was not as great as the effort required to move the house.

They moved the house a few feet at a time and stopped to regain their energy. There are few teams that could sustain a heavy pull for more than a couple of minutes. With a large truck or tractor, the feat could have been accomplished in a few minutes but would not have been as interesting. Anyway there wasn't a heavy tractor available.

All the spectators had different stories to share when the men came home from work. No two stories were alike, nor did any of them capture the true sense of the event.

As I recall this was the last house moved in the neighborhood. Houses were built, remodeled, bought, and sold but no more were ever moved from one location to another. The previous house moving had occurred about five years prior to this one. We were not fully aware of the historical significance of this event but can now look back on it as the marking of the end to old fashioned draft horse work, at least in our *barrio*.

Tom continued his garden plowing business until his death some years past his 70th birthday. I do not know who bought the team but they disappeared shortly after his funeral, as did his old wagon with steel wheels. It was a trusty, dependable vehicle that on many occasions transported kids coming home along the highway. I was one of the fortunate ones offered a ride on several occasions. In that era the Sears Farm Catalogue sold such wagons as well as harness, stock tanks and other farm implements. These items are still available somewhere at farm stores but are different from those in this age.

Today draft horses appear only in contrived events where the teams pull a heavy sled or demonstrate the driver's skill in handling an eight-horse hitch pulling a stylized beer wagon. Children today see draft horses pulling large wagons on television or in Denver, at the National Western Stock show, an annual event in January.

THE FLOOD IN THE POTATO PATCH

Sometimes, boys will do a good deed.

In our case, well, we sort of forced it on ourselves.

But it was a worthwhile achievement, nevertheless.

It happened in the spring just before the summer when rains pelted the *barrio* more than usual.

Boys always welcomed the rains. That's because that was when areas on the east part flooded and generated a lot of mud and debris before receding.

For us, this was a time to take washtubs and float in the floodwaters—usually a brief but highly enjoyable trip. Many mothers were dismayed to find not only their washtubs all muddy but also their barely recognizable sons who had floated around in the muddy waters.

I do not recall any girls having participated in these events. Chalk it up to stereotypical gender roles and/or better sense. As everyone knows, boys and mud seem to attract each other. This attraction continues until girls start attracting boys and then mud loses its mystique.

On one occasion, the flood was larger than on previous occasions, rising to a depth of over two feet in an area where potatoes were planted. The flotilla that appeared promptly when the rain slackened unceremoniously wiped out the potatoes.

The makeshift boats scraped away the potato plants.

The owner would not have been amused and would have chastised the participants severely but he did not get home until later in the day and by then we were all out of the flood area.

In an unprecedented act of kindness all the kids that had floated in the potato patch graciously volunteered to help the owner replant.

We received martyr points for helping an elderly citizen repair the damage, damage that we had inadvertently caused

Of course, he did not know who had damaged his potatoes, only that some neighborhood kids had done a good deed. No one ever told him anything about how the damage occurred and he would likely still think that the flood did it without help from a bunch of kids.

PAVING THE WAY

My hometown of Pratt, Kansas is one of a few cities where its main street is still paved with bricks.

Shortly after the first road was completed with bricks in Ohio in 1893, cities throughout the country relied on brick layers for what was considered the way of the future of road construction.

In my hometown, that job belonged to a resident of our *barrio,* Juan C. Throughout the 1940s and 1950s, Don Juan made sure the brick lined streets in our town were in good shape. He was the last of the paving brick-laying artisans working on city streets.

And, unfortunately, he never passed his special skills to anyone in the *barrio.*

Neither his stepdaughter nor his stepson showed any interest in learning how to keep streets smooth. At that time women would not have been hired to do that type of work so any interest on her part would not have had positive results or gainful employment.

Consequently, most streets in Pratt today are topped with the more economical asphalt materials or concrete.

Today these brick paved streets have fallen into disrepair, as have the Main Street businesses and virtually everything else.

While Don Juan was alive, streets he paved and maintained were level and easy to drive on. At that time there were no potholes on Main Street and it was worthy of the county seat or even a historical site.

While Don Juan was quite popular in the *barrio,* his wife Juana, was an overbearing curmudgeon. I say this, even though she was related by birth to a former wife of a grand uncle in my family. The family disposition on her side must have exhausted all grace by the time she and her sister came along.

Unlike other older women in the *barrio*, she was rumored to smoke a lot and gossip constantly, and if she ever uttered a good word about anyone, few people heard it.

The couple lived in a two-room house, which, given the occupancy rate in other homes, would have made it palatial based on the square footage allotted each family member in those days.

The stepdaughter lived with her mother in Chicago but spent part of the summer with them. The stepson occupied a room attached to the garage and lived there year round.

The family car, a sleek Plymouth, was noteworthy in that it had "freewheeling", whatever that meant. I was not aware of any other car around that had that feature. Don Juan drove the car to and from work daily and to church on Sundays, trips of only a total of four miles or so. Someone got a good deal–at least on the low mileage—when he sold it.

Rumors about witchcraft surrounded the woman of the house, Juana. The Doña was used with her name, but was largely undeserved since it is a term of respect. Her sister Martina also failed to deserve this title, but she did not live in the barrio so it won't really matter.

Juana did not mingle much with other women as she lived at the south end of the barrio. And, besides, she was not invited often to soirées or other functions among the women.

Don Juan, on the other hand, spent his only day off, Sunday, like most men in the *barrio*, listening to whatever was on the radio. During football season he listened to the Green Bay Packers games when available.

Don Juan remarried a couple of years after the death of Juana. His new wife was a very pleasant middle aged woman who had grown up in Arizona. She told horrifying stories about discrimination against Mexicans in the mines and all the towns that she had lived in. She kept house and had no vices.

Her younger sister often visited her and spent most of one summer with her. She came to keep her company following Juan's death and stayed for quite a while. Her son, "Seve", short for Severiano, played baseball on the same church team that I pitched for.

During my mother's funeral, I heard that Seve had bought and moved into Don Pancho's house around 1995. Seve's mother was a distant niece of Doña Mariquita, Don Pancho's wife. By that time, both had been dead 20 or more years, so no one knows who may have been involved in the transaction. Don Pancho and Doña Mariquita had no known heirs. And, then again, perhaps Seve's mother was their heir.

TRAGEDY IN THE BARRIO

Tragedy struck our *barrio* on more than one occasion.

This particular time it hit the family of Don Mónico—for the second time.

He was an older man who married a much younger woman who bore him one son and three daughters. He lived across the alley from us at our old house, and was the man who hired Tom and his team of horses to move his house.

Don Mónico drove a trash truck for the city sanitation department. He came home for lunch every day and had the habit of allowing one or more of his young daughters to hitch a ride on the truck as he drove from the alley into his yard.

One this fateful day, as the youngest girl tried to jump on the stirrup on the side of the truck, she slipped under one of the rear wheels. She was killed instantly, to the shock and dismay of all witnesses and those even who only heard the loud cries of horror.

Her mother ran out of the house, picked up and held her daughter to her bosom and cried hysterically. All witnesses knew that the daughter had died instantly, long before an ambulance arrived.

This was a tragedy for the whole neighborhood. This same family had suffered a house fire years before, but there had been no loss of life at that time.

The victim's sisters had a trash mouth vocabulary that they utilized at opportune and inopportune times.

When one of the nuns from the church came to comfort the family the day following the tragedy, one of the girls muttered something that ended in an "itch" sound.

What she said referred to someone's illegitimate ancestry but the poor religious sister thought that the girl wanted a sandwich. No one dared to tell the nun the truth and the mother hastened to shut the kid up. The foul mouths were in action on several other occasions but eventually the girls seemed to outgrow their tendencies toward vile speech.

AN UN-NEIGHBORLY FAMILY

Not all of our neighbors were neighborly.

Such was the case of the family of Don T.

His stepson fitted the description of a scoundrel rather well.

When the young men in the *barrio* were in the military during World War II, the stepson was home. He, somehow, evaded the draft.

That was just the beginning of what raised many eyebrows. While the war was in full bloom in Europe, he managed to secure government funds for an adult basic education program.

The problem was there was no education program and there were no students. Some residents in the *barrio* learned, after the fact, that they had been listed as students.

The local priest and a medical doctor were among those who were listed as students.

For more than a year he continued to receive funds—all on the profit ledger since there were no classes and no expenses that anyone could ever pinpoint.

Don T sired five sons on his own and three daughters. All three daughters died from a mysterious liver condition. This disease did not strike their brothers.

The second oldest son dropped out of high school twice, both times immediately following football season. No one knew when he attended grade school or junior high school but he turned up at the high school to play football. He never finished high school, actually never finished his freshman year, but was still able to secure a good job in the big city. He retired after 24 years of employment and receives a pension.

He has since suffered a stroke and can barely walk, talk or feed himself. His wife must care for him to a high degree. He once was a healthy young man who took up boxing and got into good physical shape.

Son Number 3 served three years in the state reformatory for boys, and after his release, moved to Phoenix, Arizona. He too has retired and at latest report, still lives in that area. This one was a bully in his youth. We used to call him *El Sapo,* not that he looked like a frog, but he was, shall we say, chubby. He was a classmate of mine in kindergarten but not after that.

Later in life, after moving to Arizona, he suffered severe wounds, several stabs, and cuts on his back. This happened shortly after he was released from the reformatory. According to his brother, he had gotten into trouble in his new home city. This last event served to finally get a message to him, and he heeded it by "getting religion" and becoming a better citizen.

I found Don T very interesting. By the time I was old enough to focus my attention on most of the *barrio* citizens; Don T was spending most of his time tending a garden, which he watered with water from an old rickety wooden windmill. He spent a lot of time lounging around the house. The word in the *barrio* was that he was blind, but the neighborhood wags had other ideas.

"He's not totally blind. Look, he knows where every plant in his garden is located," were popular explanations.

It didn't take me long to find out that Don T had been a victim of a railroad accident that had also severely injured my granduncle Esteban.

Whenever folks talked about the accident, they inadvertently got excited and blurted out:

"He blew up a steam locomotive."

The way the conversations went, it sounded like he had planted a bomb and blown up a train. Co-workers and witnesses to the event figured that Don T must have injected cold water into a nearly dry boiler. Whatever he did generated an enormous amount of pressure, which literally blew up the locomotive.

My granduncle Esteban was on top of that particular engine taking on sand. He was blown off the top of the engine and landed in a cinder pit several yards away and was severely injured.

The railroad policy at the time was that an on-the-job injury guaranteed the person a job for life. Life expectancy was not long in those days.

Tío Esteban had scars on his face, neck, hands and back for the rest of his life.

He had a job for life but retired a few years later. Don T retired on disability.

There was no written record assessing blame for the explosion. He ended his career around the same time that a minor trunk railroad known as "el Anton", but actually the Chicago & Northwestern or something in that vein, went out of business in the early 1920s, exact date unknown. These two events were not related and the timing was coincidental.

His wife was a strong woman who put up with the family, a disabled husband, and the vicissitudes of life. She found solace in the one room "mission" in the barrio where Sister Hughes and her husband, who played the violin boldly, conducted services on some Sundays. The rest of the time, the building was not in use.

She kept house, watered or swept the yard, a custom prevalent in many barrios were there was no groundcover in the yard and this kept down the dust. Without these measures, dust would permeate everything. Memories of the dustbowl days were likely still fresh in everyone's mind. Her stoicism was reminiscent of the Spanish form which is known throughout the world.

She was much kinder than anyone else in the family, and overall was a decent person. Her good qualities overshadowed any shortcomings she might have had. She was generous, and fed hobos who came through the neighborhood seeking a meal while traveling by freight train. Others in the barrio also fed these unfortunates who had nothing and were hungry. Many times these persons would chop wood or do other chores in exchange for their meal.

Like most other kind persons in the barrio, Doña C would pack a sack lunch for the wanderer so that he could eat another meal while traveling. She was quite different from the rest of her family and had developed her good qualities despite her surroundings. These qualities were not visible on her children. She did not drink or smoke, a noteworthy example for the rest of the family since they all did.

Only one member of the family progressed beyond the freshman year in high school but all the males obtained jobs that paid fairly well considering their limited reading ability and educational level. The only record left of the old folks in this family is an ornate gravestone in the local cemetery. The gravestone, of recent vintage, shows Carmelita 12/31/1922 – 1/12/1987 and Tomás 3/7/1880 – 9/10/1972. This gravestone replaced one that was formerly there and was much smaller and less ornate.

CRUISING DOWN MAIN STREET

By the end of the 1940s and the beginning of the 1950s, I, like most teenagers was looking forward to graduating from high school and leaving town.

Where we were all going was uncertain. A few talked of college. Most of us were ready to make to make an appearance at the armed forces recruiting station.

But before that fateful day, we wanted to make a statement in town.

This usually consisted of nothing more than cruising or dragging downtown—all ten blocks long. Most other small towns were experiencing this same phenomenon.

We did not have to file an environmental impact statement nor secure a parade permit to do so. We were usually under subtle surveillance. Most days this activity did not draw much attention from the local police as everyone engaged in the activity, including a couple of us barrio dwellers.

One particular Sunday a friend and I were cruising in his sister's car which bore out of town, out of county plates. As we drove on Main Street, we noticed that a police car was following us. After two round trips, the officer pulled us over to the curb on the north end, which was close to our residential area.

The officer was friendly but asked questions that seemed a little odd at the time: "Do you boys live in Wichita?"

"No."

"Do you boys work in Wichita?"

"No."

Finally, he got around to his real question which concerned whether the vehicle might be stolen. When the driver informed the officer that he was driving his sister's car and that she did live in Wichita, the officer retreated.

My guess is that he finally thought that car thieves would not be so brazen as to drag Main Street in a stolen car. He still took an interest in the car because of the brown faces of the occupants and would likely not have noticed much had the occupants been wearing white faces--notwithstanding the new car.

HOW NOT TO BE IN THE LOCAL NEWSPAPER

During one of my last years in the *barrio,* I was on the front page of the local paper.

Well, not exactly me, but my car.

By that time, I was a teenager and I had saved enough money to buy a used but good-looking two-door Plymouth. It beat my old pickup truck, which did have a compound low gear. This meant that whenever I got stuck or had a hard time getting the truck started, I could put in compound low gear, pop the clutch and get out and push it until it started moving and then I could get back in.

Until I told my family, I was the only one who could tell that it was my Plymouth pictured on the front page of the local daily.

On the previous day, our area had been hit with more than two feet of snow that pretty well paralyzed the town.

The local newspaper ran a photo of a car (mine) buried in a snowdrift, a couple of feet off the major highway, at our end of town. The car was totally buried and from the photo no one could tell what the car looked like, much less where it was or to whom it might belong. The plow that had come north on the highway had buried my car which was a few feet from the right of way. Driving home the previous night I was not able to get to the street in front of the house.

It took several days of melting before I was able to dig it out and managed to finally drive it out without serious damage.

In any event, this was one of the worst storms that we had suffered in many years. If the snow had been this heavy in previous years, I am not sure I would have been able to dig a car out.

Despite the storm, there was no school holiday. There was no such thing as snow days since most kids walked to school anyway. The Catholic school, where most of the *barrio* kids went until graduation or discontinuation, already had many religious holidays so we could not afford to miss any more classes. Even an "Act of God" was not sufficient to generate a "snow day" at a religious school. Too bad it wasn't an obscure saint's feast day which we could have celebrated for the first time ever. By this time I was not in the Catholic School so it would not have affected me directly.

I kept thinking that even if classes had been cancelled, we would not have found out. There were no telephones in the *barrio* until the late 1940s or early 1950s, depending on whether the household actually needed one and could afford a party line full of nosy listeners.

There was no television station that could inform anyone about weather or anything else. If there had been, no one had a television set anyway. The local radio station was a sundowner that only operated during the daylight hours. Other than country and western music, the station did not delve deeply into cultural affairs.

PART FOUR

FEAST DAYS AND FOOD

We didn't need an excuse
to celebrate in the barrio.

No necesitábamos razón
para celebrar en el barrio.

FEAST DAYS

We didn't need an excuse to celebrate in the *barrio*.

We celebrated the national American holidays, of course. But there were also happy celebrations, both sacred and secular in the *barrio* and the community at large.

Other celebrations were seasonal and coincided with saints' days.

The 4th of July was a major celebratory day as was Memorial Day.

Mexican holidays also generated music, food and gatherings both in the *barrio* and in cities where larger crowds attended dances and/or programs appropriate to the occasion.

October 12 was an important holiday, *Día de La Raza,* or Columbus Day as celebrated in the present by the Italian community.

Today there is so much controversy regarding Columbus that many cities face large protests from coalitions of American Indians and Hispanics. Some cities have threatened to discontinue Columbus Day parades and community celebrations and leave the celebrating to the Sons of Italy or other groups. This will likely not happen despite the high cost of protecting protestors and parade marchers, since it is considered a First Amendment issue. Thus far no Hispanics or Indians have boycotted the Knights of Columbus.

In an earlier era the day was recognized as an important holiday because it connected the New World with Europe by blood and culture. Mexicans and other Latinos trace their lineage to the *Mestizaje,* the infusion of Spanish blood with the Indigenous peoples. While there are those who claim direct lineage to the royal family of Spain, most of us have roots in the New World, and whether others wish to acknowledge their heritage or pass as something else is between them and their conscience. Assimilation is generally complete for later generations, a transition that started in my generation but was not finalized.

CHRISTMAS AND TAMALES

To this day, I love holidays. Whenever I think of holidays, my mind goes back to Christmas, the *barrio* and *tamales,* somewhat in that order.

It seemed to me that there could not be Christmas without tamales. Oh, I know, it happened in other parts of the country and certainly in other parts of the world.

But not in our *barrio*, not in our family.

La Tamalada was a ritual that started several days before Santa Claus made an appearance. Incidentally, with the war in Europe and everyone skimping on one commodity or another, the old bearded one had trouble finding his way to our *barrio* in those days.

Christmas was special, nevertheless.

Making *tamales,* at least in our family and *barrio,* was a production worthy of every detail.

The first part of the preparations included selecting the ears of corn, whether corn from our garden or purchased at the nearby elevator or from a farmer renowned for growing good edible corn. The purchasing part belonged to the men since they were usually the ones who drove. Then next step was the cleaning of the husks and shelling the corn.

My grandmother María or great aunt Preciliana prepared the corn for cooking.

The preliminary steps consisted of thoroughly washing the corn and heating a huge amount of water in the "wash boiler," or another large utensil. The corn was boiled in water with lime, not the fruit, the chemical, a white powder.

When the corn had burst open, it was considered cooked and then the cooks cleaned it after it had cooled sufficiently to handle without getting burnt. The cooks washed the cooked corn several times to be sure that it was perfectly clean. The cooked, cleaned corn was then set aside for further processing.

Meanwhile, the cooking crew prepared a red chile with pork in sufficient quantities to make several dozen tamales. The mixture simmered for hours before it was properly cooked. Our family almost always cooked pork loin or shoulder but tamales can be made with most edible parts of virtually any animal. Venison or armadillo tamales are common in south Texas. The aroma and taste of the red chile could be described but not in terms that would be understood by others whose imagery is based on different adjectives.

After the cooking and cleaning of the corn, the men would then come into the process again. Their job was to grind the corn with a hand-cranked mill. The sleeve, a tall metal cylinder on top of the mill mechanism, would hold about one half gallon of corn. This was the assignment for the grinder, usually my father. My younger uncles, Tíos Emilio and Epifanio also would join in the grinding, and in later years, I would get in on this activity. I don't recall whether my younger brother, Manuel, got to grind corn as he was five years younger and would have reached grinding age about the time I left for Navy flight training. There was no particular aroma associated with this phase of the preparations.

Next, it was time to prepare the *masa*, the savory dough that covers the meat of the tamal. This involved combining the finely ground corn with lard that had been creamed. There was no *masa harina* available at the time, which is the already prepared masa found in stores today.

Finally when the *masa* was ready and the *hojas* (corn shucks) were thoroughly washed and still moist; almost all preliminary preparations were finished.

The next steps usually took place on Christmas Eve prior to the family outing to Mass at Sacred Heart Church held at midnight and called M*isa de Gallo* apparently in honor of the rooster that crowed at midnight. The women would take over this part of the process, sometimes with the help of *comadres* or other neighbors, as the assembly of tamales began in earnest.

The all-woman assembly line was a thing of beauty and efficiency with the first in line arranging the corn shucks and passing on to the masa spreader. The masa spreader ensured that each shuck had the proper amount of masa spread uniformly on the corn shuck. (The masa spreader in this era was a person. In the modern era it is also a utensil or tool made of plastic that can be used like a spatula and allows a person to spread the masa more evenly.) The next step involved the addition of the pork chile in sufficient quantities to cover the masa but not too much so as not to leak out the sides of the *tamal.*

(Note: The spelling "tamale" in use today on many menus is incorrect.)

Once all the tamales were smeared and folded, the first load was stacked in the cooking utensil. The tamales were not placed on the bottom of the utensil but rather on a rack to keep them out of the water on the bottom. After filling the utensil, the lid was put on and the heat produced steam to cook the tamales. The cooking took several hours and if the cooking started around 11 p.m. the *tamales* would be ready when the family returned from Midnight Mass. This part of the preparations had a mélange of aromas and even sounds as the fire crackled and the steam erupted nonviolently from the top of the cooking utensil. The odor of chile and spices filled the warm kitchen and some escaped out through the door as people came and went in and out.

Even though we usually ate a couple of hot tamales after mass, the main meal was not until noon on Christmas Day.

While it may still be possible, it is very difficult for only two people to prepare tamales in the old fashioned way. Formerly it was a social event in preparing tamales and the actual eating was a feast.

In the modern era, *tamales* are available from a variety of sources and can be thawed and warmed, if frozen, or simply warmed a bit and eaten fresh. While the majority of tamales available commercially are not as tasty as those we made the old way, they are much easier to get to the table.

But I still miss *La Tamalada* and all the sounds, smells and activities. The conversations during every phase were a means of catching up on the events of the day, the weather, comparisons about the amount of snowfall in the "old days" and news of the new additions to the population.

This was a family and neighborhood social event filled with laughter and warmth from the people as well as the stove.

This ritual has changed in the last six decades—at least for my family. When we have a family gathering these days, we frequently buy tamales and use the preparation time for socializing and conversing rather than working on the many details of *tamal* preparation. Of course, the participants are of a different generation and somewhat removed from the original traditions.

Many varieties of tamales are available locally these days, including the traditional red chile tamales, green tamales, cheese tamales, beef tamales, chicken tamales and other types.

Notably absent are the sweet tamales that had raisins, anise, and, sometimes piñón or other nuts. These were not folded like the other tamales but rather assembled like a small pouch tied with a small piece of corn shuck. I have not eaten any sweet tamales in many years. Equally absent today are chiles rellenos with meat but that is another feast.

My mother and grandmother also made *sopaipillas* on special holidays like Christmas and almost always for New Years. Their sopaipillas were made into small squares or triangular shapes and then fried. Sometimes we added brown sugar and cinnamon, but most of the time we ate them just as they came off the frying pot so they were not as sweet as *buñuelos*.

NEW YEAR'S EVE

New Year's Eve was an exceptional holiday. I suppose it was because there was a different kind of excitement that was culminated by a celebration that literally exploded into the night's sky.

What could be better than a full stomach with once-a-year delicacies and fireworks that came twice a year? July 4th was the other, of course.

To this day, I associate *pozole*[29] and *buñuelos* with the last day of the year.

Pozole was usually served at the evening meal. How good—I mean really delicious—the *pozole* was at that time depended on another *barrio* event, the butchering of the family's pig, which, in most instances, meant saying goodbye to an animal we had fed and watched it grow up and fatten.

Butchering hogs was a colder weather event when the meat could cool quickly. If we had butchered a hog that year, this meant that our *pozole* had pig's feet and other parts of the hog.

If, on the other hand, there had not been a pig to slay, then the *pozole* would consist of only of corn that had been harvested in the fall and allowed to dry into large kernels and store bought pork.

The sweet aroma of the corn being boiled would fill the kitchen and spill throughout the house very early in the day. Drawn by the smell, sometimes, I would watch as my grandmother and mother would then add spices, garlic and oregano that included *ristras* of *chile* (red *chile* in today's world). Our family never added green chile to our *pozole* although this version is very popular in New Mexico.

Pozole is sometimes associated with a very popular Mexican stew called *menudo*. Some claim that the menudo will help overcome hangovers from New Year's Eve and other drinking celebrations. It is available today, both fresh and canned, in many grocery stores that cater to the burgeoning Mexican population.

I didn't care for the smell of the *menudo* then and don't care for it today, so I am not going into additional details.

Just after sundown, the sweet smell of cinnamon, brown sugar and flour would take over in the kitchen. A glow would come over my grandmother's face as her hands, first with open fists, and then clinched fists, would battle the tan dough into balls the size of a small orange.

My mother would then take over and roll the dough into large pancakes that went into hot lard. Once cooked, the *buñuelos* would be covered with the brown sugar and cinnamon.

(This delicacy was our dessert once a year and once a year only. I'm not sure why this did not occur at other times of the year but perhaps it was too labor intensive to do more regularly.)

Then, after what seemed like an eternity, I would watch as the grownups drank their coffee and relived the fortunes or misfortunes of the year that was about to end.

I would know that midnight was near when my father and uncles would get up to get a rifle and shotgun.

Then at midnight, at precisely midnight railroad time, the bells and whistles from the nearby roundhouse would sound followed quickly by the blast of the shotgun and the rifle. Fireworks also would lighten up the night until all the fireworks were gone.

Inside the house, the women would smile broadly, shake hands and usually hug each other and perform other good wish activities.

The men would just shake hands in a strongly manly manner and hug the children who were still awake. In some households, residents ate the twelve traditional grapes following the old Spanish custom.

I had just gotten used to the celebration when World War II broke out and the celebrations stopped.

Fireworks were precluded from celebrations because of a distinct lack of fireworks and the fact that nights were meant to be dark during the war years. Blackout conditions and the presence of a B-29 base nearby fostered the darkness.

The firing of guns, rifles, pistols, and even shotguns, was, or seemed to be, a custom brought from Mexico. Lucky for us, these were times when the setting in the *barrio* was not congested. Firing a gun into the air would have little or no danger of having a bullet come down on someone. In today's congested cities, a shot fired straight up could still come down on persons or property and cause damage. If a person happened to be at the spot where a bullet fell, it could spoil their whole day and maybe even end their life.

In a happier and less hostile era, guns, firecrackers, high-flying pyrotechnics and other noisemakers were expected, shared and appreciated.

The nostalgic sounds are pretty much gone forever but they livened up New Year's celebrations for us. These sounds are among the things that we miss now that steam locomotives have disappeared from the railroad along with other sounds that are a thing of the past.

CHILE NOT CHILI

I've often heard that a meal without *chile* is not really a complete meal.

This was certainly the case in our family. I can't remember many meals that did not have *chile*. Suffice it to say that chiles constituted a very important food in our diet

Chiles were harvested in the fall in the *barrio* when the peppers were ripe and the final harvest when they were turning red. We made *ristras* that were hung on the sunny side of the house. As these dried out, they became lighter and easier to handle. One of the tasks, assigned to my brother and me, was to hang the *ristras* out in the morning and retrieve them in the evening. The *ristras* dried in the sun for several days, sometimes a couple of weeks.

After that, we stored the *chiles* in an old wooden caboose that someone in the family had purchased years earlier. We were lucky to have that old caboose. Most families stored the *ristras* in the kitchen between the stove and the kitchen wall.

Ristras could, conceivably, last forever.

Today, I see *ristras* as holiday decorations rather than as food. Back in the days I'm describing, they were an integral part of the diet. Any dish involving red chile depended on the family reserve of *ristras*.

Chile is a necessary ingredient for dishes from *carne adobada* to *tamales*.

Chile de ristra required several steps before making its way to a meal as a sauce. My grandmother first took the *chiles* from the *ristra*, and then after washing the chiles with a damp cloth she split the chiles and removed the seeds. She removed only the seed not the veins along the sides of the chile since these contained the "heat" in the chile. The chiles then went into the oven and toasted for a few minutes and finally were ground, either coarse as chile *caribe* or fine like chile powder. The red chiles could then be used for a variety of sauces. They were a staple for enchiladas, tamales, and many other dishes.

Since refrigeration had not made its way in full force into the barrio, we had few methods of preserving the produce from our garden. In addition to making *ristras* with the ripe red chiles, we also pickled green chiles in quart or half gallon jars.

This process was fairly straightforward but the actual recipe varied from one household to the next. First in our recipe the chiles were soaked in brine for two to three days, and then they were washed again and arranged in the jars along with onions, garlic and assorted spices, including oregano and a dash of olive oil. Many families added carrots, cauliflower and other ingredients that they liked in their jars.

The jars were boiled, steamed if the utensil was more airtight, for more than an hour and then allowed to cool. The lids were then tightened to create an airtight seal. These jars, prepared in the fall, were not consumed, in our house, for at least two years to allow the flavors to mingle and the ingredients to properly age. The jars were stored in boxes in the storm cellar where the temperature was fairly constant throughout the year. The temperature never reached the freezing point down there so things were safe from freezing.

Yet a third method of preserving green *chiles* was to roast, peel, and string them into *ristras*. As these chiles dried, they turned black and hardened. In the winter, we soaked them in hot water before using them in several dishes. Reconstituted, these *ristras* yielded salsa as hot as that made the previous summer with the green chiles freshly roasted and peeled. This particular salsa was very hot and had a unique flavor.

The family also preserved other vegetables and fruits

Jars of fruit and tomatoes, which are actually fruits, were consumed during the winter following their preparation. I remember adding sugar on top of these tomatoes to make a dessert on occasions during the winter when the supply of fruit had been exhausted.

Canning peaches, pears, and tomatoes was usually reserved for the women in our family. They also made jelly from plums, which grew wild in the Sand Hills west of town and near the local cemetery. In other areas like New Mexico, and Colorado, Chokecherries are used for jelly and wine.

LA CUARESMA

La cuaresma, the 40 days of penance observed by most Catholics, (Lent) was a distinct time in the *barrio*.

No, not because we looked forward to giving up candy or the weekend movies, but because this was the time in which my mother and grandmother cooked dishes reserved for this season only.

If New Orleans was celebrating Fat Tuesday, we certainly didn't know about it in the *barrio*. Every Ash Wednesday, the start of Lent, my mother would take us to Sacred Heart Church for the early morning Mass and the priest's thumbprint of ashes to our forehead.

It was understood that this was a season in which we were to give up some of our simple pleasures such as candy and movies. We also were to reduce our foul language, which we did.

We limited it to our thoughts, which we eventually had to admit to in the confessional.

These were also the days of fasting—for adults—and meatless Fridays.

In the absence of meat, we had *torrejitas, nopalitos* and *quelites*.

Let me start with the *torrejitas*. This delicacy was our version of the pancake in that the final product resembled the pancakes of today. Unlike pancakes, the ingredients include only eggs but no flour, and a bit of baking powder. The batter was then mixed with dried shrimp or mashed cooked potatoes could be dipped into this batter and also fried.

Dried shrimp was a mainstay during Lent in the *barrio*.

The *torrejitas* include the egg batter with cheese in the mashed potatoes. These patties were also served with a red *chile* sauce.

Nopales and quelites were also standard fare, but these were usually not available in Lent since it falls during the winter months.

Nopales are, as the name suggests, cactus.

The young tender, cactus were gathered carefully from pastures or roadsides. The spines/needles were cut off and the cactus was washed then cut into small pieces and cooked.

The resulting foodstuff was sort of stringy and appeared somewhat slimy to the unaccustomed palate. Nopales when fried with scrambled eggs were tasty and not slimy. Nopales were also preserved in jars but the crop in the spring and summer was not always worth preserving.

Quelites are another story altogether.

As children we could all head for the ditches next to the highway or adjacent to country roads and pick *quelites*. These plants were a form of wild spinach, or so we were told. They resembled very closely weeds that were not edible and may have been poisonous.

At the time, anyone in the *barrio* could have gone out and gathered *quelites* with little thought about getting the wrong weed and making someone ill. Today I do not think any of us former *quelite*-gatherers could safely gather *quelites*.

We also had *capirotada* during lent. This was a bread pudding that my mother and grandmother made and served as a dessert. The main difference between the bread pudding made today and the *capirotada* of the time is that it contained piloncillo, unrefined brown sugar made into the shape of a cone. This dish too varied among the families in the barrio.

The Mobile Market

Our *barrio* was so isolated and poor that there were no neighborhood stores or *tienditas*. Although in the past, as remembered by the old folks, there had been thriving businesses there.

So the stores came to the *barrio* in the form of a mobile market, so to speak.

Three or four times a year we looked forward for the old and semi-decrepit panel truck with Don Arturo at the wheel.

An older man, Don Arturo sold condiments such as, *comino*, cilantro, oregano, dried, ground, red, *chile*, dried shrimp, chile *piquín* and other items of interest to *barrio* folks

This method of selling Mexican ingredients predated the availability of such items in supermarkets. Back in my youth, few sources for Mexican ingredients existed, thus Don Arturo had a good market for his products not only in our barrio but elsewhere.

He had no regular schedule for visiting our area but came around periodically.

Don Arturo supplied us with these necessities for many years until one year when he did not show up at all. We later learned, through the migrant folks who worked seasonally in his home area that he had died.

No one carried on his work, servicing his established route, which may have covered the middle part of the state. By this time there were some ingredients available in the supermarkets in adjoining larger cities where the population of Latinos had increased.

Along with the increase in the population, there had been an increased demand for the items that were previously available only from Don Arturo. I never learned his surname, only his *nombre de pila*, Arturo.

The Watermelon Man

By 9 o'clock on most Saturdays during the summer, the *barrio* folks were in their front yards looking toward the horizon to the north.

We were looking for and waiting for the Watermelon Man.

We referred to him only as "Mr. Wood," and in the *barrio* vernacular, he was *El Señor Madera*.

He drove what we thought was an old Buick Roadster convertible and pulled a rickety trailer full of watermelons, cantaloupes, cucumbers, squash and other vegetables.

He was a crusty old guy, bald and tall. He wore a tank top, actually an undershirt that accentuated his hairy shoulders and back. It might appear that all the hair growth genes had forgotten his head and concentrated their efforts on the area exposed by his shirt.

He was a white person but had a dark tan from working in the fields and apparently from wearing the undershirt in the hot sun rather than a long sleeved shirt.

He traveled to the town on Saturdays during the season when his produce was at its peak. He always stopped in the barrio on his way to town since we lived at the north edge and he had to go by there to get to town.

We were good customers for his cantaloupes and watermelons. His prices were low and we got the pick of the crop since we were among the first customers.

He raised yellow meat watermelons, something that few other farmers could do successfully. Currently there are watermelons with yellow meat in the supermarkets but these do not compare with those that this man brought to the barrio.

Even though my uncles raised cantaloupes, these were never ripe before Mr. Wood's trailer hit our *barrio*. We did not have good luck growing watermelons and there was no way to compete with Mr. Wood's crop, which thrived in his sandy soil.

Unlike Don Arturo, who drove a panel truck that exuded class, Señor Madera's vehicle was old and a model no longer produced on the assembly line by any automaker of that era. It had no top and the back seat was usually filled with straw and his prized melons.

After the barrio folks had bought a sizeable portion of his produce, he went on into town where he set up his produce stand in a vacant lot at the north end close to the ice plant. By noon or no later than 3 p.m. he had sold out all his fruits and vegetables.

We all knew approximately where he lived some 18 miles northwest of town, but no one had ever visited his farm.

Following his death, the barrio lost both a friend and a reliable source of excellent produce. Everyone thought that he was an old bachelor who had lived alone on his farm all his adult life.

I was surprised to learn, years later, that one of his granddaughters had married one of my high school classmates. No one had ever seen anyone related to Mr. Wood and he had never mentioned any family.

Maybe our assumption was wrong. And then again, maybe not.

Outside help

Most other produce sold in the barrio came from out of state.

Occasionally a truck from Colorado with a load of potatoes or pinto beans would show up and sell these from a street corner or from a vacant lot on the edge of town near the barrio.

Beans were a staple item for most of us so buying a 100-pound bag at that time was not unusual. A 100 pound bag of potatoes was a different matter. Potatoes do not keep as well as the dried beans. Potatoes were plentiful and available year round so it was not necessary to stock up for the winter. Ten pound bags were almost always available in the grocery stores and lasted long enough to not go bad before they were all used up.

Other produce for our family came from Tío Zacarías' and Tío Esteban's gardens. They cultivated several varieties of chiles, yams, tomatoes, onions, garlic, *calabazas*,[30] corn and some herbs.

Tío Esteban gardened on a smaller scale. His plot was next to the larger one and did not contain as many items. Both plots were watered with excellent well water, which reached the plants from the windmill via long, large hoses. These two uncles also sold *chiles* as their reputation for raising hot, tasty and meaty chiles was widespread.

PART FIVE

THE END OF AN ERA

The only place left where I can still recognize the names of old friends is in the cemetery.

◆

El único lugar en que puedo hallar los nombres de mis viejos amigos es el camposanto.

Unwelcome return

When I departed the *barrio* to serve my military duty in the U. S. Navy, I thought that perhaps I might return and work for the railroad in a lucrative position.

It seemed to make a lot of sense at the time. Prior to this time, I had attempted to secure a good job along with many of my high school classmates. These young men had hired on as brakemen or firemen and were drawing a good salary, among the best in town.

Even though I had worked for the railroad on the "Bullgang" at the roundhouse for around three years during the summer and early fall while attending school, I was refused employment in the operating union jobs.

I was shocked to learn that the conductor and engineer unions would not allow persons of Hispanic descent in these lucrative jobs. For many years these positions were filled by generations of immigrants from places that provided German, Polish, French and Greek surnames and others of unknown origin.

It became painfully clear that I would have to emigrate elsewhere to find a higher paying job than might be available in my hometown.

In my hometown, the bulk of the population consisted of retired farmers and businesspersons whose goal in life was to pay minimum wages and charge high prices. They had made their fortune and were determined to keep others from making one. There were many retired railroaders who remained in town but others fled to Florida where there was no snow.

Following my Navy service, I returned to college via the University of Kansas and obtained my degree. Despite the two years of Junior College that I had prior to returning to school, it took two and half more years to graduate. I had more college hours than most juniors but actually entered the university as a sophomore.

After graduation, I became a teacher, not realizing at the time that some menial jobs on the railroad paid as much or more. Nevertheless, I continued my involvement in educational endeavors for over 50 years.

THE LAST FAMILY IN THE BARRIO

There is only one family left the *barrio* from the 1940s.

I last saw them in 2000 at my mother's funeral.

This family was among the lightest skinned in the *barrio*. They were originally from New Mexico and may have been descendents from the original Spanish settlers with no ties to Mexico. There was no trace of *Mestizo*[31] in them, unlike the majority of the others, who were somewhat darker complexioned.

The family lived in a modest house with two large lots surrounding the house.

The head of this family was Don Pedro, who was better known as "Pete."

He worked at the local cemetery, most likely in some supervisory capacity, for local folks said that was the only way he could afford his old Ford pick-up with a V-8 engine. Most vehicles in the barrio had the traditional in-line six cylinder engines and not a lot of power.

Don Pedro had other distinctive qualities including the fact that he furnished his garage for dances at no charge. He had the only garage with a concrete floor in the *barrio*. After he died, the weekend dances ceased, not because of his death, but because there was no one available to play for the dances or to dance.

Don Pedro and his wife, *Fina,* had two daughters and two sons.

The oldest son was legally blind and attended the School for the Deaf and Blind in another city after a few years of struggle in the local schools. The younger son was many years younger than the rest of us. He finished high school around 1959, years after my younger brother graduated.

The two girls in the family attended school periodically. Neither one finished high school or ever pursued a career. Both pursued young men and married while in their late teens.

The older daughter has been widowed for several years. She looks almost exactly like her mother did in her 50s. She has been widowed for more years than she was married.

The younger daughter married a man 15 years her senior and is now divorced.

Only the two sons and their families remain in the *barrio* today. When I last saw the family, the younger son was working for the post office, with more than 30 years of service. The blind son was teaching at the community college and doing well.

Their mother, *Fina,* continued to live in the same house until her death a few years later.

I still have fond memories of the family. For example, part of their property served as an athletic field for the boys in the area. Girls at this time did not participate much in athletics either in school or on the playground.

One of the older neighbor boys built a pole-vaulting pit. He vaulted about three days per week when the weather permitted it. He used an old bamboo pole and could vault more than 10 feet. Today with fiberglass poles and other modern equipment both men and woman are able to vault over 16 feet. For that time, a 10-foot vault by a boy with no coaching and poor technique was pretty good.

Other interesting facts associated with this family are also part of my memories. In this case, it was their extended family that people in the *barrio* simply took for granted as *la gente de Nuevo Mexico*[32].

This included John and his wife, Zenaida. He was not a Baptist but rather a rogue. His wife was a sickly woman known mainly for her nickname--*La Lala*. When someone referred to her it sounded like they were trying to sing a song.

She hardly ever went outside and never went far from her house or her sickbed. She ailed for almost all the years that I lived there.

He, on the other hand, was seldom at home, preferring to cruise the neighborhood and visit others.

Their house sat on a large lot, which contained two outbuildings, the local mission and the omnipresent outdoor toilet.

This couple also had a well, as did all the barrio residents. Theirs, however, did not have a windmill or simply a hand operated pump. They were into the mechanical age with a small motor that pumped the water. Their pumping mechanism made a funny noise as the electric motor moved the pump up and down. If it was equipped for manual operation, it was never used in that fashion.

If the electricity happened to fail, they could not draw water. When the city installed water lines into the barrio, they refused to install a tap. Finally, years later they installed indoor plumbing but still used the well for drinking water.

The only record left of them shows that he was a World One veteran born 2/22/1891, died 7/21/1961. She was not a veteran of anything in particular but was born 3/20/1901 and died 7/15/1978. Their marriage was in accord with the pattern of the times, older man, younger wife widowed young.

CHANGES IN THE BARRIO

Many conditions have changed in this land and in the *barrio*.

The plots of ground containing the history of former occupants are still there but the barrio no longer exists on land. It only exists in the hearts and minds of former dwellers, or perhaps, their descendants.

In my childhood, it did not take a village to raise a child but the *barrio* did provide an environment that fostered good behavior and citizenship.

Everyone knew everyone else, and any transgression by a child resulted in a report to the parents, who took corrective action. The phrase, *le aviso a tu mamá*,[33] was sufficient to straighten out any kid.

Villages no longer participate in the rearing of children, but all manage to support at least one idiot.

The changes that have occurred since the heyday of *barrio* life are visible to those of us who survived, but hardly noticeable to anyone else.

For example, when Tío Zacarías died in 1946, the family had a wake for him. The Mexican style wake, an around the clock event, was a far cry from the Irish wake of literature.

The scene of wake in the *barrio* is one that will always stick in my mind. First, there was the body in the open casket in a room in the family's house. All the furniture in the room had been removed and members of the deceased's family and friends could come at any time and offer prayers, mourn in crying whispers and offer condolences.

Outside in the back yard, men shared stories and passed around a bottle of spirits to the memory of the deceased, of course. Perhaps because the sight of a casket in the otherwise empty room brought unwanted chills and fears they didn't dare to face, children always found a reason to also be outside--and always seemed to find some type of game to play.

Inside, the women prayed, updated relatives on their families, shared a tear or two and took their turns in the kitchen for the endless meals. In inclement weather all activities took place indoors. The kitchen was unusually crowded on these occasions.

After a sleepless night for all, the hearse came to the house and moved the body to the church for the Funeral Mass. Following the Mass for the Dead, the funeral procession proceeded to the cemetery where the priest recited the usual prayers, some with audience response. After the mandatory *Polvus est et Polvum Remeters* or words to that effect, the casket was lowered into the grave, and the sprays of flowers were left on the casket.

By my high school years, burial customs had changed to where no one in the *barrio* actually had wakes at home. When someone died, if, the family was Catholic; they had a rosary and visitation in the mortuary chapel. The following morning the priest celebrated the Funeral Mass and conducted the burial ceremony. If you happened to be an Alter boy and served at a funeral mass, you normally got a couple of dollars from the pallbearers.

The end of the wakes at home also brought to a close a special social event that allowed relatives, friends and neighbors to catch up on family activities. It was an occasion where family members from distant places came together even though it was not a joyous event.

In my mind, one of the reasons for the change in this custom in the *barrio* was the fact that certain residents were not well liked by many of the other residents of the barrio where everyone knew everyone else. Or, perhaps, the deceased had no known relatives, so there was no one to conduct a wake, or if there was one, few people came.

Another reason could be that relatives and friends lived in other cities and many times were notified of the death too late to attend the service.

From the old days when a meal was furnished by neighbors and friends of the family and served in the home, we now see a luncheon catered by the women of the church. In small towns this meal will likely be held at the Knights of Columbus hall or the parish hall.

The majority of barrio people were Roman Catholic, so most of my memories center on the rituals and rites of the church.

I witnessed more than my share of burials when I worked for the cemetery digging the grave and covering it after the graveside ceremony. The end of the funeral was fairly similar for all denominations.

Today's funerals are still emotional but less personal. Many times the minister or priest does not even know the deceased and relies on family input for words to say to the bereaved and the congregation. Obituaries in the local paper now carry information on minority folks, something that rarely occurred in the 1940s, at least in our town.

END OF AN ERA

When the railroad started scrapping steam locomotives, it signaled the demise of the local roundhouse, a four-stall leftover from previous glory days when according to those who remembered, it had 12 stalls. The railroad had been the chief employer for residents of the *barrio*.

In my own family, the railroad had employed a grandfather, two granduncles, two uncles, my father and me.

Opportunities for gainful employment faded as the railroad pulled out and relocated its operations. Fewer trains ran as schedules were cut back.

We watched in anguish as the daily schedule of around 20 to 30 passenger trains a day during WWII, was reduced to only four, later two--and eventually none.

Passenger trains operations virtually ceased in the 1950s.

The cutbacks by the railroad also resulted in upheaval to the *barrio*.

Those who worked for the railroad, especially in the roundhouse operations, had to either relocate or find other jobs. After investing more than 35 to 40 years, a few men decided to follow the job out of town and to commute home on an irregular basis.

Others put their homes up for sale but the economy did not support any real estate sales. Families were stressed as a direct result of this and some divorces occurred, none in our family though.

In our family, it seemed like time and neglect finally wiped the last building from our family complex. Tío Emilio eventually rented the main house, where the old folks had lived, to a young man from the barrio. He and his wife both failed to take care of the property and it decayed rapidly.

The reason for the speedy downfall of the old house is quite interesting. No one would have thought to just cut a hole in the roof in order to install a television antenna, but this guy did. The rain coming into the attic eventually seeped into the house and pretty much ruined it.

He moved out after getting far behind in his rent payments. After that, no one else could or would rent it. That's when we advised my uncle that it was time to tear down the old homestead. The hazards were just too much since electricity was still hooked up and the walls and the roof were ready to tumble.

Today there are no buildings in this compound. It is merely a vacant area that consists of two lots on which we pay property taxes to the city and county. Even the stately tall trees are gone. The lots do not reflect anything of what used to be there while we were growing up.

As railroad operations dwindled, the number of residents in the barrio declined. Today there are fewer than five families living there. Only three or four individuals are descendants of former residents and have continued to live there.

Entire bloodlines are gone. The only place left where I can still recognize the names of old friends is in the cemetery. All older relatives are there permanently as are all of their old neighbors.

There is still a segregated section with recent burials of "colored folks" that I knew as parents of schoolmates. Now schoolmates' names are the newest additions to these gravesites.

There is very little left to show that this *barrio* was once an enclave of folks from all strata of society. Most came from across the Rio Grande fleeing the Mexican Revolution. They adapted quickly and provided defenders of their new country during two world wars and additional skirmishes not classified as wars.

They also provided dependable, conscientious workers in a town where for many years they were not readily accepted and not welcomed as customers in most of the local businesses.

Despite all these obstacles, some of which endure to this day, there were families that produced academic overachievers and youth that have done well in the majority society.

From our family alone, there were four members who earned master's degrees and one Doctorate.

Our family placed a high value on education and our father and mother pushed us to go to college and achieve. No one else from the *barrio* had even finished high school except for our mother and her two brothers, my younger uncles.

Our immediate family produced four educators.

Visitors to the *barrio* today no longer can see many vestiges of the bygone era when it was a flourishing community.

Houses have been torn down and vacant lots mark the site of previous abodes of our *vecinos*.

For someone who lived there, it evokes memories of what used to be, and I can still picture our old neighbors and remember activities in which they were involved. Most of the residents had an influence on the remaining survivors, whether it was as a role model or a horrible example not to follow.

The remaining memories will die like the *barrio* did unless someone chronicles them. There are many stories of life in the *barrio*, and these exist today only in the memories of the remaining few former residents like myself. If more of these memories are not written and preserved soon, they will fade even more and will eventually be lost. My generation is the last to recall much about this era. If we don't write it, it will be lost forever.

This is my contribution as I remembered it.

To quote a popular saying in the *barrio:*

He dicho.[34]

But, perhaps, better said:

¡He escrito![35]

EPILOGUE

Acculturation has become a two-way exchange in that we accept the language and most customs of the mainstream culture while foods, festivities, and cultural events that we grew up with, are now accepted in the mainstream culture.

Up to now virtually everything of interest to north of the border Mexicans has been adopted, or perhaps, co-opted in the U.S. by non-Latinos.

First our food became mainstreamed to where there are numerous variations of what attempts to pass as "Mexican food."

Later *señoritas* caught the attention of young and old White males.

Lastly *Salsa*, the dance, came into vogue and now U.S. folks consider most things of Mexican origin as everyday things. Sandals and *Guayaberas* are mainstream clothing and straw hats, possibly Panama Hats, are widely popular.

The presence of so many Spanish surnamed baseball players has brought about a different attitude toward the general group. There are even movie and rock stars of Hispanic heritage. There are Hispanic owners of major league teams, as well as players and managers.

At age 12 when I first started playing competitive baseball, there were no other *barrio* boys in the league. I played American Legion Baseball for four years and maybe set the scene for the modern Hispanic stars now in the major leagues, but perhaps not. In any case, there have been Hispanic/Latino professionals in several sports besides baseball.

There have even been Hispanic players inaugurated into the football hall of fame. Former players have become coaches so there has been a presence at different levels in professional sports. Boxing has always had more than its share of Latinos in its ranks. Today there are even few notable professional bull riders, many Brasileños and a few Spanish Surnamed riders.

Tennis includes Latinos in the ranks of the best players, both men and women. Soccer, which is becoming more popular in the U.S., calls on the talents of Latinos from other countries as well as native born athletes.

We have more women who have broken into the basketball ranks than men.

If we Hispanics are going to be the majority minority group within the next few years, we will have to produce more athletes and politicians in order to reach parity.

FORMER RESIDENTS LONG GONE

Names of old time residents include the following who were family members.

María Palacios Maldonado, 8/15/1885 – 10/30/1960
Preciliana Palacios Chabolla, 1/4/1876 – 8/27/1960
Zacarías Chabolla, 1878 – 1946
Celedonio Velos, 1892 – 5/2/1922
Manuel M. Maldonado, 1867 – 1927
Antonio Chacón, unknown
Silverio Cobos, 1854 – 1926

These old-timers include grandparents on my mother's side and their relatives, many of whom I never actually knew since they were deceased before I was born. All maternal uncles and their wives, my aunts, are buried in the local cemetery. Both parents are also there. With these family members is buried much of the culture that existed in the *barrio* and the history and memories diminish with each passing year. Maybe some of them will live on in these words now on paper.

RFV 2007

ENDNOTES

[1] *Barrio* as used throughout this book simply means neighborhood, my neighborhood

[2] The terms Hispanic and Latino were almost interchangeable by the beginning of 2006. In the 1940s, we were referred to as Mexicans because our ancestors came from Mexico. Today's Hispanic/Latino population encompasses people from Central, South and North America.

[3] The term *güero* meant a light-complexioned individual

[4] The time of the Mexican Revolution is generally placed at 1910-20.

[5] *La Prensa,* which literally means The Press, was published in Spanish in San Antonio, Texas in the 1940s and had a national audience as evidenced by my uncle as a subscriber. In 2006, *La Prensa* is published bilingually and also an Internet edition. Major U.S. cities like Los Angeles and New York City have daily and Internet editions in Spanish.

[6] Windmill

[7] The word *chile(s),* which stands for peppers, is often Americanized as *chilli,* which is wrong.

[8] *ristras* are peppers tied together in a string to dry out and preserve.

[9] The term *altar boy* was used in reference to boys who assisted the priest during the sacrament of the Mass. In 2006, girls now also serve in this capacity.

[10] *compadre* and *comadre* are very popular terms in the *barrio* and refer to individuals who serve as godparents in the Catholic sacraments of Baptism Confirmation, First Communion and Matrimony.

[11] There is more than one version of the story of *La Llorona.* One popular version tells of a woman who is always crying after her child drowns in a nearby river.

[12] *Adivinanzas* are riddles and games that are as popular today as they were in the 1940s when there was no television. *Adivinanzas* can be found on the Internet. There are several books on this subject.

[13] *cuentos* are stories, generally children's stories.

[14] *Sobrenombres* are nicknames.

[15] *Lonas* was a popular term used to refer to someone wearing overalls, which were made out of canvas material.

[16] *Huerta* is a large vegetable garden and sometimes also used to refer to an orchard.

[17] Literally translated, *Caraveo* means good-looking.

[18] Chet Atkins is known as "Mister Guitar." He was an accomplished musician by the time he graduated from high school in 1941.

[19] Andrés Segovia is a world-renowned player of the Spanish classical guitar. He was born on February 18, 1894 in Spain and made his public debut at age 15.

[20] French term for the carefree enjoyment of life.

[21] *Caldo de res* is a popular soup made of beef and vegetables.

[22] *Matamoscas* stands for killer of mosquitoes or fly swatter.

[23] The Mexican Revolution.

[24] colonel

[25] sergeant

[26] The Persians, not really their background.

[27] *Carne adobada* is meat marinated or rubbed with spices and red ground chile and used often in a specially-prepared pork stew.

[28] *Las Posadas* is a Christmas tradition practiced today in Latin America and in this country in which neighborhood youngsters (and adults, too) play the role of Mary and Joseph seeking lodging.

[29] *Pozole* is a very popular Mexican stew. It derives its name from the stew's main ingredient, which is dried white corn processed with lime. Some prepare the dish without meat.

[30] Squash

[31] A person of mixed blood.

[32] The people of New Mexico.

[33] "I am going to tell your mother" or "wait until I report this to your mother." Regardless, the intent was to drive fear into the accused child.

[34] What I have said stands.

[35] This is what I have written.

About the Author

Ramón Francisco Villarreal has devoted more than half a century to helping the under privileged get ahead in life through a better education.

His latest effort, *Recuerdos de mi Barrio,* while a personal memoir, is also a historical view of life in a poor neighborhood in rural Kansas in the 1940s and the lessons he learned of how to overcome life's day-to-day obstacles.

What he learned most from those struggles—and triumphs—was that the path to success is through education. "The one thing that my parents engrained in us was that you never stop learning and that we were going to go to college," Villarreal recalls vividly.

Fortunate for the Villarreal children that included a younger sister and a younger brother, their mother was the role model they needed to lead the way. Their mother, Doña María Nieves Maldonado de Villarreal, was not only the sole female high school graduate in the *barrio,* but also the only one who later attended college and who eventually obtained more than one degree and became a teacher with a Masters degree. Ramón F. Villarreal learned well. Education has been his lifeblood.

He is currently the director of the Interwest Equity Assistance Center (EAC) at Colorado State University (CSU). The Center is one of ten federally funded centers that provide technical assistance and training to school educators in their respective regions. The Interwest EAC is based in Denver but attached to the CSU School of Education. The program provides him so much comfort and pleasure that he says:

"I have no notions of retiring again until and unless the federal funding dries up."

He retired in 1999 as an investigator and manager in the U.S. Department of Education's Office for Civil Rights with more than 30 years of federal service. The weekend after his official retirement, he went to work for the Center.

His service to the advancement of civil rights spans more than fifty years. Along the way, he listened patiently to the complaints from students, teachers and administrators and community persons when he worked as an equal opportunity officer, a racial dispute mediator and as a trainer for three other federal agencies in Texas.

"I have experienced discrimination in many forms throughout my life, both private and professional. I have been active in working for equity and putting an end to discrimination on whatever basis it may exist," he says bluntly.

He is a member of the League of United Latin American Citizens (LULAC), the American G I Forum, the Colorado and National Associations for Multicultural Education, Associated Directors of Bilingual Education, and recently completed a three year term on the Steering Committee (Board of Directors) of the Association for Gender Equity Leadership in Education. In 2006 he received the highest award bestowed by AGELE, the Shirley McCune award for contributions to gender equity.

He has been a high school teacher, a university professor for Kansas University Extension, and a visiting teacher for summer sessions at the *Escuela Normal* in Saltillo, Coahuila, Mexico. Villarreal graduated from high school and Junior College in Pratt, Kansas after graduation from 8th grade at Sacred Heart Catholic School. He served in the U.S. Navy as a NAVCAD and later as Airman. He earned bachelors and master's degrees in Spanish and Education at the University of Kansas.

He lives in Denver with his wife, Sandra also a graduate of Kansas University. They have two children and five grandchildren.

.

www.ingramcontent.com/pod-product-compliance
Lightning Source LLC
Chambersburg PA
CBHW020914290526
45784CB00002BA/545